A General Guide to Filling Your Garden with Plants on a shoestring.

Andrew M Molloy.

Copyright © 2017 by Andrew M Molloy. All Rights Reserved.

No part of this publication may be reproduced, distributed, or transmitted in any form or by any means, including photocopying, recording, or other electronic or mechanical methods, or by any information storage and retrieval system without the prior written permission of the publisher, except in the case of very brief quotations embodied in critical reviews and certain other non-commercial uses permitted by copyright law.

ISBN: 9781521444627

CONTENTS

Title Page
Copyright
About the author.
Also, by Andrew M Molloy.
Foreword. 1
The basics. 3
Planning & Collecting. 17
Problems, Pests & Diseases. 30
Planting Guides. 46
Herbs. 53
Hazardous & Poisonous plants. 56
Vegetables & Fruit. 60
Cuttings. 67
Cold Frame as a Nursery. 70
Fertilisers & Uses. 74
From the Author. 78

JANUARY.	80
FEBRUARY.	93
MARCH.	104
APRIL.	114
MAY.	123
JUNE.	131
JULY.	138
AUGUST.	146
SEPTEMBER.	152
OCTOBER.	156
NOVEMBER.	161
DECEMBER.	166

ABOUT THE AUTHOR.

Andy was probably born with green fingers! He has always had a passion for gardening, wildlife and anything to do with the natural world. He has interests in, art, macro-photography, writing and gardening. If you would like to know more about Andy, you can follow him on Goodreads, and ask him questions about his books on Goodreads, http://www.goodreads.com/AndrewMartinMolloy

Andy also writes under his pen name Joe KING. http://www.amazon.com/author/joekingplanetxxx
Which he uses to write horror, sci-fi and some of the strangest, and funniest stories that you are ever likely to read!

If you do find this book helpful, then do please leave a review. I personally read them all and will always strive to make improvements to my books wherever possible. Many thanks and happy gardening, Andy.

http://www.amazon.co.uk/hp/B071ZTM5FK UK

http://www.amazon.com/hp/B071ZTM5FK US

ALSO, BY ANDREW M MOLLOY.

A General Guide to Filling Your Garden with Plants on a shoestring.
A General Guide to Filling Your Garden with Plants & Wildlife on a shoestring.
A General Guide to the Gardener's Year.
The Wonder of Trees.
Climate Change: You, and your Garden.
Your Garden for Free.

FOREWORD.

Modern life has no doubt changed from the times when our parents used to grow fresh vegetables and raise their own plants. We tend to have less time for our garden and spend more time working than ever before. It can be tricky juggling everyday life, but with some effort and a little planning, your garden can look amazing. The hard landscaping in your garden lays the foundation, but what do you do then! Maintenance and keeping your borders looking fresh may seem a never ending and expensive choir. That need not be the case. With growing the right plants, in the right locations, you could easily fill your garden with seasonal flowers and vegetables. It does not matter if you are a beginner or a seasoned expert, no one person could know everything about this vast subject on plants and you don't need to be. Growing your own plants can be as simple, or as complicated as you choose to make it. This guide will talk you through how simple it can be to fill your garden with plants, but let's not stop there. If you have been wondering why you don't get much wildlife visiting your garden, that can be one of the simplest things to change. All creatures depend on some form of plant. Just by choosing the right plants can attract some of the most amazing butterflies, birds and the multitude of wildlife that is out there into your garden. If you think filling your garden with plants is impossible on a shoestring, think again. You too could be soon enjoying a wonderful garden filled with plants, for less that you might think. Plants can be expensive, but with some money saving tips, this really is simple to do for anyone wishes to have a garden that not only looks great, but will reward you with fresh produce, flowers and wildlife.

It can be daunting organising your garden through the year, so I have included some bonus material at the end of this e-book to give you some idea of what is possible, and the month by month jobs that can be done throughout the year.

THE BASICS.

Do not be one of those gardeners that rushes out each spring or summer and buys baskets full of plants, then just digs a hole in the ground and plops them in, and wonders why later, when the plants have performed badly. It is not that you cannot grow them, it is because you have not done your preparation. Soil conditioning is really not that bad to do and can be just as rewarding as the results you will see later in the year. Plants are just like people; we need some basic requirements to survive. Thinking about your plants this way may seem odd, but by doing so will give you more of an understanding about what they need, and less likely that you will neglect them. Most of what a plant requires is common sense. You wouldn't go all week without drink water or eating. Plants are no different. They need watering and feeding for them to do well and by adopting a regular routine of just looking at your plants, you will soon learn by just looking at a plant what it requires. Again, plants are just like people, when things are no going well, we show signs of being ill. If a plant is wilting, you don't need me to tell you it needs watering, but the signs cannot always be apparent, so I have included a section in, Pests and Diseases, to give you a better understanding of what to look out for, and the signs a plant can display when it is not doing so well.

The first thing you need to look at is your garden aspect. Each garden is different, and it may sound obvious, but you need to see how much light your plot is getting before you go out and plant hundreds of plants and seeds. Then be disappointed at the poor show they give you when you realise, they needed full sun and you have planted them in a shady, poorly lit area. It's not rocket science, and you do not need a compass and a fancy camera light gauge metre. Just go outside and look. If you are new to gardening and have just moved into a new house, this will be essential, because it will determine the plants you grow. Ideally you would do this over the year and see where in your garden you get the most sunlight and which parts are shaded, but with a little knowledge on the sun's arc through the year it will save you a lot of time later on deciding the best spot for your planting. At midday on a sunny day just look at the position of the sun, and do not look directly at it at any time of the year for obvious reasons. It does not matter what time of year you do this, because it will give you a rough idea of where it will be in the height of summer when its heat and light will be the most intense. If you are fortunate enough to have a large garden, then in some respects this not as important, because you will have plenty of sunny areas, unless you have numerous large trees surrounding your home, but if you have a small garden. This is very important to maximise your plants potential. Remember that fence's and large shrubbery can also affect the light levels of your garden, so take this into account when you decide on where you would like the plants to go.

Once you have a rough idea on the sunny spots and the shady areas, then it's time to look at your soil. If you are fortunate to have well managed loam rich soil, then great, you are half-way there already, but like a lot of gardens. It is normally clay, or sandy soils that need to be worked on to get the best out of your plants. The ideal soil type would be clay loam rich soil and if you do have this, consider yourself extremely fortunate, because it is more likely a previous owner has done all the hard work for you, or you are in a part of the country that this soil is prevalent.

Clay soil is a double-edged sword, because some plants will thrive on it, like roses, but in general it is difficult to work and sets like concrete in the summer. On the plus side, it can be nutrient rich, unlike sandy soils which freely drain and are normally nutrient poor, but as a personal choice are preferable to the latter, for the less back breaking work of digging them over.

It is a simple task to determine what soil type you have. Just grab a hand full and squeeze it in your hand and have a look at what it does. If it clumps together and feels waxy and smooth, then it is a good possibility you have clay soil, and if it falls apart and is crumbly, then the opposite applies, and it is probably sandy soil. You could go out and buy a tester kit to check the PH levels, but the point of this book is to save you money and with just a little feel and a look. It is not hard to see what type of soil you have. It is also a good idea to look at your neighbour's garden and see what plants are doing well, because it can be a good indicator of soil type and PH level. A neutral PH is favourable, because you can grow the widest range of plants in this, because a lot of acid, or alkaline loving plants will tolerate this soil type.

Chalky soils can also cause problems and in extreme cases, it is better to work with what you have rather than spend time and money on improving a soil type that is just too extreme and will keep reverting to type, but do not be put off. There is a plant for every condition, and if all else fails, then you can always grow the plant you have always wanted in a pot and keep it happy by giving it the right sort of compost it requires. If you do feel your soil is extremely acidic or alkaline, then I do recommend you test the PH levels and you will have to decide on your next approach on whether to try to redress the balance, or to choose

A GENERAL GUIDE TO FILLING YOUR GARDEN WITH

plants that prefer these conditions.

If you are keen to get going, whatever the time of year Then it is best to check the ground the day before and if you do have clay, and it's set like concrete. Then get the hose out the day or evening before and give it a really good drenching, but not too much so that it leaves it waterlogged, but just enough so that you reduce the workload on yourself when digging over the soil. It would be preferable to get all this done during the late autumn to give the winter frosts time to work on and break up the soil for you. If, like many of us the thought of going outside digging over a clay bed in the freezing cold has kept you indoors, then that is okay, just wait for a nice sunny spring day.

Do not be dis-heartened by having to dig and prepare large areas, because you do not have to go out and do this all in one go. Little and often, is the best way forward and if you are not used to this workload, then do any large areas over several days. There will be plenty of time to get your borders ready for the new year ahead during those nice days in late autumn and early spring. So do not panic and think you must rush out and get this all done in one day. Be patient and only do as much as you feel you are able to do, and you will soon have them looking great and ready for the year ahead.

In an ideal world we would all have composting

areas and in a large garden you will definitely need an area for the volumes of waste material you will have during the growing season, because your green recycling bin will not cope, and will soon be overflowing. If you can accommodate a composting area, then great. Choose a place where it is out of view from your main garden and with some recycled pallets strapped together, you can soon be making your own.

Pallets can be easily found in recycling centres, building sites, skips and internet free giveaway sites. Be polite and ask. Most people are more than happy to get rid of them, because it costs them money to dispose of and if necessary, offer a couple of pounds for them.

Once you have sourced your pallets and have decided on the spot you want your composting to happen, just simply turn them on edge and with a length of string (bailing string is ideal for this and is very strong and long-lasting) tie them together forming square boxes, with two or three sections. One is for new waste material, and once this is full, start the next and so on. Periodically turn this over to ensure all the materials are broken down and if you have, ideally three box sections. The composting material can simply be dug over into the adjoining section of your compost heap. Try to ensure you have variety in the materials you use and avoid woody materials as they will take longer to rot down and you will end up with poor results. Needless to say, do not put in food waste, like meats or food you have cooked, because this will attract vermin, but do put in vegetable peelings and salad trimmings.

Also, let us not forget leaf litter. This material is readily available in Autumn and breaks down very quickly. It is ideal for mulching and suppressing weeds, keeping moisture in the soil and a great conditioner and more importantly, it is free.

Do not worry if you have a small garden and cannot accommodate a composting area, because your green recycling bin should be more than adequate to dispose of the annual waste materials.

Your soil can never be underestimated, and if your plants are to grow in abundance, then you are going to need to dig in some organic matter to keep it nutrient rich and healthy. Any organic material is going to improve your soil, and a really good tip is to not throw away spent compost that you have had plants in from last year. Instead, tap the plant out of the pot that you are disposing of and shake out the roots. Leaving just the compost behind, and dig this into your borders, but do check for pests within the compost and discard it if present. It may not be packed with nutrients, but it will help to improve the structure of the soil and enable organisms in the soil to feed and create a better environment for your plants. Conditioning your soil is a long-term investment and will not happen overnight and when you see a neighbour's garden, that is flourishing. That has not happened in an instant. It has taken years of adding organic matter and feeding the soil, but do not be put off by this. A garden evolves over time and yours will too. Patience is the key to gardening, and with a little effort you will soon be on your way to having an eye-catching display.

Nature is a wonderful thing and when your garden is plagued by it, she can do it on an epic scale. If you have just moved into your new home and are looking at a garden that is crammed full of bramble and nettle you will understand what I mean. Weeds are the gardener's nemesis, along with pests, again. Don't be put off by this because the solutions can be very simple, and we will go over the ways to tackle these problems in the following chapters.

Annual weeds are relatively simple to tackle, you grab a hoe and sever them from the surface and it's that simple. If you want to, they will pull up easily, because they do not have the established root systems of perennials and are generally growing from seed laid down from a previous growing season, or if you have recently dug over your soil. Then you will get a flush of weed growth from seeds that have lay dormant from years ago, just waiting for their time to grow when the conditions are right to germinate.

Perennials on the other hand can be a nightmare

A GENERAL GUIDE TO FILLING YOUR GARDEN WITH

to eradicate, but with vigilance and persistence you can eventually rid your borders of these. You have two choices here, and it's a personal choice of mine not to use chemical methods to solve this problem. Firstly, this book is to save you money and for me it is a moral issue that we are all responsible for our environment. In this day and age of people having less time to spend doing what our parents did on a daily basis, we tend to these days look for the easiest way to do something, and not necessarily the right thing. Using chemical treatments needlessly, when we are destroying so much of our planet, is something we all can do to help. I do state that this is my own opinion, and everybody will have to decide what path is right for them. If you do decide to use a specific chemical treatment, then please. Read the instructions very carefully and take the necessary precautions with your health and safety, and do not apply these in the presence of children or animals. Secondly, my method on perennials is a full-on assault. When you dig over the soil, remove as much of the plant roots as possible and if you are fit and able, then double digging is a good and sure way of getting deep enough to remove the roots, but even then. You will be surprised how deep a well-established bramble, or at worse, Japanese Knot Weed can be, so be prepared to dig. If your borders have not been turned over for years, this will help improve their structure and also air-rate the soil. Do not be tempted to put these roots on your lovely new composting heap because they will regrow and contaminate the compost. Either burn them safely or put them in your recycle bin. A small compost heap will not generate the heat that is required to kill the roots, unlike on a commercial scale. Once you have done the hard work of removing the perennials, be assured some will still grow back and it would be foolhardy to think you have seen the last of them. But once this first dig on virgin soil has been done the worst is over, and any new weeds that emerge will pull up easily and in no time at all you will be free of them. Do remember though, even with a chemical treatment you're still going to have to dig over the soil, so is it worth it? I will leave that thought with you to decide. If you do happen to have Japanese knot weed. Then be prepared for a long battle, because they are deep-rooted and hard to eradicate and will test your patience to the limit, and have even been known to push through concrete, but again, it is your choice of treatment. It is one of the very few circumstances I would understand that a person has had no choice, but to use them.

Organic materials like horse manure is gold to any gardener and in my experience well-rotted mature is not too bad if the smell bothers you, but once it is dug in the smell will soon go, and as you would normally do this in late Autumn or early Spring, any odour should not bother you too much. Do not be tempted to put fresh (Green) ma-

A GENERAL GUIDE TO FILLING YOUR GARDEN WITH

nure on your garden as it will leach out nutrients as it breaks down and can harm your plants. It is best to dig in well-rotted manure in the late Autumn along with when you are digging over the area you are working on, but do not worry too much if you cannot get hold of this, because pelleted chicken manure is a good alternative and can be simply scattered over your planting area. If you can get hold of manure all the better, as this is the best bulk organic material, you can put on your garden and will work wonders with your soil. Look online and in your local papers and you should be able to find a local farmer that sells bags of it, reasonably cheaply and will be worth the investment or better still. Look for a local livery yard and ask them about their horse manure, and in a lot of cases they will be glad to get rid of it, and if necessary, offer a few pounds. It will be worth the effort later on. A word of caution on this particular source of manure. Check to see if they are using straw or shavings, because you do not want a wood shaving mixed manure. They take a lot longer to break down and whatever you do, do not be tempted to put them on your garden in a (Green) fresh state, because they will again, leach nutrients instead of adding them and would be better to just avoid them. If you can find a good supply of straw mixed manure, then do not worry if it is not rotted down. Grab as much as you are able, and pile it in a quiet corner of your garden and let it rot down, and next year you will have a ready supply to add to your soil.

I have only given you an outline view on soil, because at this stage I do not want you to get bogged down with PH levels and macro nutrients, etc. A good rule of thumb is adding plenty of organic matter from the few I have mentioned, and you will not go far wrong, but you will not get great results unless you put some effort into improving your soil. With freshly dug virgin soil you will find that you may have a first good year of growth, then it will be a steady decline.

If, however, your budget will not stretch to giving your borders a good feed with organic matter or you are unable to for whatever reason, then a good alternative is to localise how you add this. When you put a new plant in a freshly dug patch, then just treat that spot with a good few handfuls of whatever organic material you have, because something is always going to be better than nothing. Over time, you can slowly add more to your borders as you go, and you will be amazed what a difference this will make. Landscaping of a garden with hard structure can be done in a relatively short time, but with plants and planting, patience is the key and if your fortunate to be able to buy large specimens then great, but if you are not, then we need to give them the best possible chance. By just following these guidelines you will be rewarded with, healthy ,vigorous and beautiful looking plants that with patience and time will catch up, and will probably be better than a larger specimen you bought, because they have had time to adjust to their growing location. Unlike a mature specimen that may, or may not do well in that spot you have chosen, and will be difficult to move once rooted in. Whereas a smaller immature plant, if not doing so well, can easily be dug up and moved to a better location in your garden.

There are literally thousands of fertilizers on the market these days and if you are in any doubt about adding any extra nutrients, then read the label carefully and do not over apply these, because in some cases, less is better than more. Let us not linger with this subject too much now, because ultimately gardening needs to be enjoyable and by keeping things simple, you will enjoy it more. This next chapter is to help you decide what is best for your soil but do take caution when adding chemicals to your precious soil, because it can be difficult to correct once you apply them.

In order for your plants to grow well, you will need to know a few basics on their requirements and once you are armed with this information you will be better equipped to deal with any problems you will come across with their growth. I shall only give you a brief outline on the main three at this point, because in the fertilizer and uses section, we will go over the topic in a bit more detail.

All plants need three main elements to grow well, and they are Nitrogen, Phosphorus and Potassium better known as NPK.

Nitrogen is needed for good strong and healthy leaf growth.

Phosphorus is needed for good strong healthy root growth.

Potassium is needed for flowering and fruit production.

With good soil management, all three of these elements will be in ample quantities to give your plants the best chance of doing well, and rewarding you with healthy, strong growth and a good show. You are less likely to encounter growth, disease and pest problems.

PLANNING & COLLECTING.

All you need is rough sketch of your garden, and I do not mean go outside with a measuring tape and make an architectural drawing. Just a rough sketch to give you an idea of what you have, and where, and how, you would like to plant your garden and remember, we are not aiming to transform your garden structure, you are merely going to fill it so that you have all the plants you could ever want, at a low cost. Firstly, put in the features you have that are permanent i.e., paths, sheds and greenhouse, etc. Then add the borders you want to fill. If you require more, then think about where best to put them and if you do decide that they need enlarging, or you want more planting space, then map them out on your plan, and then in the garden when you are ready. Then set about getting these dug and as mentioned in the preparing your soil, following the simple guidelines. Secondly, and this is where it can get tricky, you want to visualise what your goal is. Do you want mainly flowers, or shrubs in your garden, or herbs, vegetables and fruits? Or as I prefer, a combination of them all. Then think back to where the shady areas are, and the sunspots are, and note them on your plan. This will determine the plants that will do well in these areas, and the ones that won't.

Now you have a rough guide to work too, and at this point I will assume your areas you want planting are ready. When planning at this stage, do take into account that you're looking at creating a well-balanced garden, so take into account a plants height and spread, because with some plants you will be surprised at how much growth they can put on in a single season and can soon swamp a border. So, when selecting a particular variety, do read the instruction on the plant label or seed packet, and another good rule of thumb is to plant taller plants at the back of a border and smaller ones at the front to give the borders a more balanced look. Colour schemes are another thing to consider. This in part, is a personal choice and only you can decide what you like, but as a guide. Try to use complementary colours to each other and experiment to see what works for you. There are no set rules on this, and everybody will have their own idea of what they like. I personally like an eclectic mix of colours, and do not forget that leaf colour, shape and size can also be important in creating a beautiful border and with the choices on offer, it can be daunting, but again. Be bold and unafraid to try new things and just add

A GENERAL GUIDE TO FILLING YOUR GARDEN WITH

new plants gradually to existing schemes to see how they look. As your experience and confidence grows, so will your knowledge on what works and what does not. A garden is never the same in any given year and change and development is part of the excitement. Another thing to consider is insects, and I would hope you will choose and incorporate plants and flowers that not only help these declining species but will also give you and your children great pleasure when you see bees and butterflies visiting your garden. Nature is a wonderful thing and should always be a part of any well-balanced garden and this may seem a large task but trust me. Just planting the right plants will have an enormous impact on your local wildlife, and we all have a responsibility to try to do our bit to help. I would not want my grandkids to never have the experience of seeing some of our beautiful birds, moths, butterflies, bees and numerous other species in my lifetime, because they are in such a decline. This is happening as you read this book, so do encourage wildlife into your garden, and it will reward you back for free.

The next step is collecting, and this is where you are going to need to do some leg work. If you can afford to go out and just buy the plants and materials you want, then that is great, but if like a lot of people. You want to, or just do not have the budget to simply go out and buy them, then this is the part of the book that for me, is the most rewarding.

A greenhouse would be ideal and if you do not have one, then you can pick these up, again from your local free advertising sites on the internet and in your local classified ads. It is a little effort to dismantle and reconstruct, and anybody can do this, because the construction of an aluminium greenhouse is simple, and designed to be that way. With a good day, or less, you should have it rebuilt and glazed. Do not worry if the glass is covered in algae or dirt, with a good clean off with soapy water you will be amazed how fresh and new it can look. I bought mine for fifty pounds and it is a generous eight feet by six feet and more than adequate for my garden, but the same again. If this is not in your budget or you are restricted for space, then a cold frame can still be productive in looking after plants and once bedded out can be easily dismantled and stored away for later use. I have written a specific section on cold frames, so do not worry if a greenhouse is out of reach for you. A good source for the materials is a double-glazing firm, and they sometimes have an onsite skip full of windows they have been removed from houses they have replaced with new ones. With a simple design you can easily construct a cold frame and have a nice hinged window but do ask first and if a few pounds are needed to be given, then it is well worth the investment. The size and design again, are up to you and the size of the window will de-

A GENERAL GUIDE TO FILLING YOUR GARDEN WITH

termine the construction, but do choose a spot where it will receive a good amount of light, and on warm days, remember to keep it open, because you will be surprised how hot it can get inside a cold frame. You do not want to come out in the garden and find your treasures all limp and gasping for a drink of water!

You can also purchase a plastic stand up version than can again, be stored away with ease during the none growing parts of the season but do weight these down or attach to a fence as they can be prone on a windy day to fall over. I would strongly advise that in order for you to fully delve into this, that a greenhouse is the best option. When you are in there, on a cold and rainy day, pottering around with your plants. You will wonder how you ever managed without it and not only will it extend the season for bringing on plants early, it is also great for growing your own summer salad crops without the worry of inclement weather.

The next thing you will soon need is plenty of is pots and when I say you will need plenty, you will need as many as you can get your hands on. One of the best places I have found is my local reuse centre and with the occasional visit. I have amassed enough for my needs, and at a fraction of the cost new. You could use anything as a container from old food tubs to the plastic trays you buy mushrooms in. Anything will do, because once the plant has grown and planted out, the container obviously will not be seen, and as your collection of pots grows. Then you can slowly recycle those unsightly ones and have the more traditional ones to give your greenhouse a more professional look. Plastic pots are everywhere, you just need to look in the right places and that can be from garden centres, to neighbours who have recently bought some new plants. So, do not be shy in asking and like the vast majority of gardeners, we are generous folk and will readily help each other, so again. Ask a friend or neighbour to not throw away pots they no longer want. I am sure once you have shown an interest, they will be more than glad to help. Also, plant swapping is another good way to build up your collection and it is always worth growing a few extra for this purpose, and once you build up a swapping network it can be invaluable in obtaining new plants.

The next step is compost and there are two ways you can do this. Firstly, the traditional route of buying seed and cutting compost for your seed planting and cuttings and then having to buy a multi-purpose compost for planting them onto. Secondly, is a less traditional way, but still effective, is to buy a good quality multi-purpose compost only route. Do look out for multi buy, offers. You will be surprised how much compost you can get through in a season. This will save you money, and a bag of compost will always be more expensive to buy as a single bag.

When sowing larger seeds using this method will not be a problem, because you can simply plant a single seed into a cell or pot of compost and cover it. The real problem is when you have seeds that are less than one millimetre and then some forward thinking is involved. Fill your seed tray or pot as you normally would, then tamp to create an even surface. You can then water the compost, yes, I said water and allow the compost to absorb the water and re-level the surface if required. Scatter the fine seeds as thinly as you can over the surface. If you have some super fine grit sprinkle this on top or if you do not have this, then using an old sieve, place some compost into this. Then dust the surface of the tray or pot, ensuring you give a thin layer of compost over the top. In doing your sowing this way, you will ensure a better and even germination and the super fine seeds won't be washed away when you water them in. This does go against a lot of gardening rules on planting seeds with seeding compost, but it works and when money is tight, it is a good second-best option, and will save you buying different composts.

The next thing you will need is seeds. Over the years you will build up a good collection and it would be wise to look after these and store them correctly. If you have an old biscuit tin, this is perfect and airtight. Also, keeping your treasures in a cool dry place, will ensure that they last for a long as they possibly can, but the first year they lose their germination capabilities, it is best to dispose of them and save further disappointments at seed sowing times.

Do not be tempted to go out and just buy packets and packets of seeds. Firstly, you will pay a premium price at a garden centre and secondly, this is where your planning comes in and some restraint will be needed, because with thousands of seeds on offer it can be difficult to stop yourself buying lots of seeds with good intentions of growing them all, then realising you do not have the space for them. So be strict with yourself and choose wisely. At this point you should a have good idea of what you want to grow, so if you need to make a list, then do so, but stick to it and over the years once you get into this more. You can gradually select more, and not like I have done in the past and have ended up with masses of plants growing away in the greenhouse, and no space in the garden for them. Although they are easy to give away, it would be better to focus for now on the things you want to grow, considering the space available you have. Lastly, on seeds. A Mecca I have found to really help build your collection are pound shops. They have a multitude to choose from and can be as little as twenty-five pence a packet. Also, keep an eye out at these outlets for bargain plants that have gone past their best and are literally giving them away. With a little TLC you can bring them back to life and feel proud you have saved the plant. You can also buy a good range of soft fruits and bare rooted plants at certain times of the year, but these can be a gamble, and are not always successful in bringing them back to life out of season. So, unless they are pennies or free, I would avoid these if you can. As the season goes by, do look out for the plant reduced sections in every outlet you visit, because some plants are perennials and although they have gone past their best and look shrivelled and dead. They are just winding down for the year and are well worth buying and kept until next year and will come back to life to give you a wonderful plant, at the fraction of the cost in its peak condition. Do read the label and if it's something on your list or just a great bargain, then do buy it. Perennials can be costly to buy, and this is because they need to be cared for, for longer by the garden centre, so if you do come across them in a reduced section. They are well worth buying and will give you years of pleasure, but again only if it's something you like and want in your garden.

Seeds can be bought anytime of the year, but do check expiry dates on marked down stock, because the seeds may have gone past their viability time and the initial low cost you bought them for, will be a waste of time when they fail to germinate.

Another way to save money, and it is the easiest way. Is at the seed planting time. One of the biggest mistakes you can make is sowing the whole packet of seed. This is where restraint is needed. With large seeds it is simple. Plant them singularly into individual pots or cells and only enough for your required space and a couple for giving away, or non-germinating seeds. Smaller or dust like seeds are where we make, and I still do make this mistake, we simply sow too many, and waste seed. It is far better to make two sowing s, than one large one. Sow the first as thinly as you possibly can and even add sand to the seeds to help to distribute them evenly, and if you find after they have germinated you do not have enough. Simply re-seed some more. Sowing times are worth sticking to and do read the minimum temperature guide on the packet, because sow too early, and it will be to cold and the seeds will sit in the pot and will most likely rot before they have a chance to germinate, and do be careful at this stage not to over water, because again, some seeds will cope with being damp and others will not, and the last thing you want is to spend two to four weeks waiting for your plants to show through and nothing happens, and will have to re-seed them again.

Another problem with over sowing seed is with your vegetable and salad crops. Things like lettuce, carrot, radishes or basically any crop you cannot harvest gradually as they produce their crop, you want to sow successively, over a two to three-week period and have a continual crop.

A GENERAL GUIDE TO FILLING YOUR GARDEN WITH

Rather than making one sowing and end up with a glut, and unable to use them all. By successive sowing you will be saving seed and money, as you will not have to go out buy these during the growing season.

Other items worth collecting are cane's and labels. Canes become useful later in the year when your plants need support, and many will. A good alternative is recycled branches from cut down trees. Obviously not all trees and large shrubs are suitable for this as they do not have straight stems, but where you can, trim them into useful straight lengths. They can be used for supporting runner beans, peas, taller flowering plants and if you are fortunate to come across them at your local reuse centre, then do buy them, as you will definitely find a use for them in your garden.

It is always good practice to label plants, and as your collection grows you will soon learn why. Last season thinking I was clever with my tomatoes, I grew five varieties and thought I would remember which is which, and when they started to grow, they all looked the same. This would not have been a problem if it was not for the fact that one variety was a bush variety, and as I could not tell them apart at this early stage, I did not know how to treat them to suit their growing needs. A bush variety needs the tips pinching out to encourage side shoots, and an upright or cordon one does not. So, it is worth doing and like I said, as your collection grows, you will need to know which plant is growing in which pot to know how best to look after them. Do not get me wrong, with experience you can normally tell by looking at a plant what it is, but it is worth doing just in case. If you are just learning about plants, this will also help you learn, plant names.

Labels can be made of any material providing it can be written on and does not rot. Lollipop sticks are good but rarely last long, and so are plastic containers, trimmed down to a label size, but do use a permanent marker when writing the label, because watering the plant can wash non-permanent ink away and after you plant out, do keep the labels as they can be used again when you grow that particular plant again.

Other accessories like twines and string you should be able to find alternatives and not purchase them new. I find bailing twine a great alternative and it costs nothing, is very strong and if you know of a local livery yard or horse owner, they would gladly give away as much of this by-product, because after they have used a bale of hay or straw, the string is generally dis-guarded.

Another good idea is to collect seed catalogue s. They have some great offers in them and will show you new varieties to look out for and offer them at great prices. Every seed company will have one, and all good garden centres will have a stack of them and are normally free. I can only show you so much within one book on plant types and species and to honest, each and every plant is worthy of a book on its own. Plant catalogues are not only good for expanding your knowledge on plant names, but they contain a picture of the plant and will show you in more detail how it will look as a mature plant. So, during you plan making phase, do go out and collect these if you are struggling for ideas, and I am sure they will inspire you as much as they have me over the years.

PROBLEMS, PESTS & DISEASES.

All gardeners at some point have had or got a pest or disease they need to tackle and again, it is my personal choice not to use chemicals in my garden. I prefer to tackle these occasional outbreaks in a natural garden friendly way. This is where I have a problem, and I have had to take a step back and really think about this section of the book. Do I arm you with the knowledge to go out and kill every bug or insect you see nibbling away on your prized plants, or do I try to impart my philosophy on life and a well-balanced garden ecosystem? Our planet as it stands, is laced with chemicals and are overused at a scale that would shock you, and as an individual we can minimise the use in our gardens. So please think twice before you go out buy and them, because in many cases, there is a friendlier way to tackle pests and disease and cost you only your time, thus, saving you money.

It may be a cliché, but there is a cause and effect happening in your garden every single time you upset the balance. Let us say you eradicated all the

A GENERAL GUIDE TO FILLING YOUR GARDEN WITH

green fly and aphids, then the ladybird larva suffers, because you have taken their food supply away and then there is one less insect species for birds to eat and so on and so forth. By only tackling what you really need to, and in a garden friendly way. You will keep this balance and be rewarded with a wider range of wildlife that I promise you, will delight you, your children and grandchildren. In turn, I hope you will pass this knowledge onto them and by doing so, help to create a small haven for a lot of native species, sadly needing people like us to keep their existence alive. If you think I am being over dramatic, then please go online and do the research for yourselves and you will see us gardeners are becoming more and more important in safeguarding our wildlife. We may not be able to stop development and our green spaces being built on, but we can look after our gardens, and you can feel proud that your part in a larger picture is being done in helping our rapidly declining wildlife. For this reason, I am only going to show you a garden friendly way to tackle the following problems you might encounter, and I will leave it up to you on how to deal with a specific pest or disease. Another good point to make, is that chemicals used in pesticides, insecticides and fungicides are always changing as we learn more on how harmful they can be to us, and our environment. As our knowledge expands, so do the products on offer and no doubt even as I write this book, some would be no longer available, and others being developed, but if you do feel the need to treat your garden this way. Then do read the label carefully, be cautious and sparing in their usage and again, take extra care if you have children and pets and please never store them where they can get to them. Ideally keep them in a locked area which only you have access to. If you do feel, after attempting to try to eradicate a pest or disease that you have no alternative to try a more radical approach. Then my advice is to take the offending insect, or where you can, the plant, or the part that has succumbed or is ailing, in a sealed container (fresh specimen) to your local garden centre, or plant outlet. Ask an adviser on your options on specific treatments, and in many good outlets they will be more than happy to give you the correct information and product, to safely tackle the problem. Also, if you are not able to handle or collect the specimen for whatever reason. Then take a good, clear picture of whatever you feel you need advice on and take this instead, because a lot of problems can look similar and you want to give any adviser the most amount of information you can to make an accurate diagnosis.

Common problems you might come across.

This topic is vast, and I would be foolish to try to explain to you every single problem, pest or disease you may or may not encounter so the best approach is to give you an overview of common

A GENERAL GUIDE TO FILLING YOUR GARDEN WITH

problems that you may encounter.

Annual weeds. These can become a particular problem on a freshly dug area where you wish to directly plant seed and can out compete your seedlings. A good old saying worth remembering is (one year's seed, seven years weed) and this is true. So being systematic in your approach and remove any annual weeds beforehand and hoe the area regularly. If you do feel that a border or large area needs a weed killer to eradicate them. Then there are numerous branded makes on the market that can do the job effectively, but prevention is a better way and with good gardening practices, by applying a mulch and regular removal by either hoeing or manually removing them by hand. Some common annual weeds to look out for are Shepard's purse, Hairy bitter cress, Meadow grass, Common chickweed, Groundsel, and Annual nettle.

Perennial weeds. These are different to annual weeds, because of their root structure. Which can remain persistent in the soil for many years and their fleshy roots, rhizomes and other storage organs cannot be easily removed with hoeing and mechanical digging. If you are only dealing with a few weeds, then a leaf contact weed killer will do and for larger areas a soil contact weed killer may be used, or you could use a selective weed killer. These should however only be used in my opinion, if digging them out first is not an option.

Once again, there are numerous products on the market for this purpose and too many to list, so it would be better for you to decide which control is best suited to your particular need. Some common perennial weeds to look out for are Ground elder, Bindweed, Creeping thistle, Horsetail, Couch grass, Colts foot, Willow herb, Bryony, Oxalis, Lesser Celandine, and some deep-rooted ones are Bramble, Dock and Japanese knot weed. Once again if you do need to use weed killers be extremely careful and follow exactly what each manufacturer states on the label.

There are times when you are going to have to tackle larger infestations that may affect your plants, but saying that, do not be concerned when you see the occasional leaf has been nibbled or you spot the odd insect among your plants. This is not an infestation and quite normal and requires you only to remove the said leaf or insect and discard responsibly. Your plants are a great indicator of what is happening to them and that can be a certain way a leaf has been eaten, or a certain part of your plant has discolouration and with experience. You will learn to look out for these early warning signs and tackle the problem before it becomes an infestation and more dramatic measures will be needed. A lot of problems can however be prevented with good housekeeping and keeping your garden tidy and free from clutter. It is also a good idea to learn about your allies that

A GENERAL GUIDE TO FILLING YOUR GARDEN WITH

are good to have in your garden and the ones that can cause harm, to prevent you from killing the ones that will help to fight against pests. Hedgehog, shrews, frogs and toads feed on many ground dwelling pests and birds, although can cause a small amount of damage, feed on the numerous insects, as do spiders and centipedes and not forgetting ladybirds and their larva, also aid in your battle against pests. So, should all be encouraged into your garden. Even wasps and ants play their part in controlling pests and where would we all be without the bees, who are amazing pollinators and a good indicator of a healthy environment. There are however numerous insects that can cause mayhem if left unchecked, like weevils, slugs, snails, beetles, sawflies, frog hoppers and millipedes, just to name a few, so learning the signs can prevent plant loss, and save you money.

Good housekeeping can never be underestimated and by doing it regularly, it will save a lot of these problems occurring and an easy way in the greenhouse, is ventilation. Wherever possible, keep the door or window open on the days the temperature is high enough to do so. If you know it's going to be a warm or a sunny day and are going to work early or you are out for the day, then do open the door in the greenhouse and cold frame before you leave, because the temperature will rise rapidly and cause your plants to wilt and suffer and a stressed plant, is far more likely to succumb to pests and disease. Good air circulation is also required, especially during the growing season and can prevent a lot of mould spores and plant problems in a closed hot, and humid environment of the greenhouse or cold frame. So again, wherever possible, keep them ventilated, allowing good fresh air flow and remember to check your plants and if any need watering do so, because they can dry out quickly and left unchecked all day, will also become stressed and wilt.

Common leaf problems.

Eaten leaves.

Slugs & Snails. Many plants will show signs of damage and you will see holes that may have been stripped in the leaf and the tell-tail silvery slime trails, so cultivate the soil regularly to expose their eggs and avoid organic fertilizers and mulches. You can manually pick these off and dispose of responsibly. More prevalent at night.

Earwigs. Young leaves are generally eaten in the summer, and they hide during the day and feed at night and a good way to control is to place inverted pots stuffed with straw or hay amongst affected plants as they will use this as daytime shelters and then can be removed and disposed of responsibly.

Woodlice. Holes can appear in seedlings and near shoot tips, but they generally eat decaying matter and are rarely a problem but can be found on plants already damaged by pests or disease so good housing keeping is advised to prevent build-ups.

Millipedes. Seedlings and soft growth are eaten, and slug damage is enlarged, but they rarely cause serious problems so to avoid organic fertilizers in areas they are known to be and cultivate soil regularly to prevent build up, because they can be a problem once established.

Vine Weevils. Leaf notches may be seen from mid spring onwards and over long periods and control can be difficult, but on vigorous, healthy plants this is generally not a problem, but do clear debris away regularly to minimise hiding places for the adults.

Sawfly Larva. Plants are defoliated. The larva is easily recognised by displaying when the caterpillar like larvae are disturbed and are easily picked off, but larger infestations may need an appropriate insecticide.

Caterpillars. Many plants can be affected from caterpillars from various moth and butterfly species and the most common you may come across are the Winter moth and Cabbage caterpillars and Webber and Tortrix moth caterpillar and control is a simple case of picking off by hand. Chemical controls are available.

There are many more Beetles and Bugs that can eat your leaves including leaf cutter bees, but unless large infestations are found simply pick off the offending insect and dispose of responsibly and if you still feel they are a nuisance then chemical treatment can be used, but if you are in any doubt do seek professional advice, and as before, collect or take photographs to show an experienced adviser.

Discolouration of leaves.

Aphids. Leaves will often be sticky from honeydew (aphid excrement) and may be blistered or blackened by sooty moulds also stems and buds may be covered. With light infestations a jet of water will remove them, or a solution of soap and water sprayed on can be effective, but left unchecked, they can multiply rapidly, and you may need to use a selective insecticide leaving most other beneficial insects unaffected.

White Flies. Several species can occur and can be found in the greenhouse and leaves can be covered in a sticky honeydew (white fly excrement) and the adults will fly off if disturbed. If infestations are low, then picked off the leaves, but larger infestations you may need to use an appropriate insecticide also insecticidal soaps can be effective, but resistant greenhouse white fly do occur.

Mealy bugs. Can occur in the greenhouse and you

will notice a white fluffy substance in leaf axils and plants may have a sticky honeydew (excrement) on them and blackened with a sooty mould and the roots can also be affected. Ladybirds are a good biological control, but if this fails, you may need to use a chemical control or an insecticidal soap.

Powdery Mildew. You will notice a powdery white growth on the upper or lower surface of the leaf from varying Fungi that can cause this and can be spread by the wind or rain splash and can overwinter on the host plant. The leaves will yellow and fall off and thrive on plants growing in dry soil. Try to avoid growing plants that are susceptible and water and mulch as necessary. Remove affected plant in affected areas straight away and if the problem persists, you may need to use a suitable Fungicide.

Red Spider Mite. You will notice the leaves become dull and increasingly turning yellow having a pale mottling on the upper surface and will drop off prematurely and can have a fine silk webbing covering the surface. There are several species with varying colours ranging from green/orange/yellow to red with black marking and are less than 1 mm in size. They can be difficult to control with more pesticide resistant strains. There are biological controls available, but for large infestations insecticides may need to be used.

Leaf Miners. You will notice a white or brown area appear within the leaf and often in character with a particular type of leaf miner. There are many varieties, and if the infestation is small then just picked off and dispose of the leaf responsibly, but if larger infestations are found an appropriate insecticidal spray may be needed.

Bacterial Infections. You will notice that various black or yellow spots appear with a halo appearance and as they merge the leaf will die and fall off. Bacteria spread by insects, rain splash or windborne seeds can cause this, so remove all affected leaves and if the problem persists then an appropriate chemical treatment may be needed.

Insecticide & Pesticide. It is worth mentioning these signs to look out for if you intend using these treatments. Discrete spots or blotches may appear and are often bleached or scorched looking which may die, but the plant will generally recover. This is usually caused by chemicals used at the incorrect ratios or applied during hot sunny weather, so only use chemical treatments when you have read and understood the instruction application.

Weed Killers. As above, this is worth mentioning if you intend to you use these controls or in some cases your neighbour. Pale and bleached spots may appear and can turn brown with bumps on the stems. In severe cases the plant vigour will be lost and can die, but in some cases, they may regrow. Spray drift can cause this when applied on windy days or a poorly cleaned watering container you have used to apply them. It again, is good gardening practice to read all the instructions on usage and application and only use equipment you intend to apply these with and apply with a drizzle bar applicator instead of a spray.

Drought. All plants can be affected by this, especially pot plant's and the first signs will be the plant is wilting and then may discolour and turn brown and eventually die. This can simply be redressed by checking plants regularly, especially in pots, with regular watering.

High & Low Temperatures. High temperatures will show as yellowing and brown patches normally starting at the edges and will be dry and crisp and affected leaves may shrivel to prevent this provide shading in a greenhouse and good ventilation and avoid overhead watering on hot and sunny days. Low temperatures will show as bleached or brown patches and may turn completely brown also flowers heads susceptible to frosts may wither, discolour and die. To avoid this, provide prone plants, especially young ones with adequate winter protection.

It worth looking out for deficiencies in your plants and in most cases, can be easily redressed and for our purposes I will list the main three

(NPK)

Nitrogen Deficiency. Pale green leaves will be seen, and these can sometimes develop yellow or pink tints and the growth of the whole plant may over time become weak and spindly. This can happen to plants that are grown in poor and sandy soils, and container grown plants. You can apply high Nitrogen fertilizers such as Sulphate of Ammonia, Nitro chalk or Dried blood to rectify the problem.

Potassium Deficiency. This can be seen as foliage may turn blue, yellow or purple with brown discolouration either in the leaf tips or at the margins and the whole plant can lose vigour and growth can be reduced. This can happen when you grow plants in soil with a light texture or with high chalk or peat content. You can improve the texture of the soil and apply a dressing of Sulphate of Potash or a high Potash fertilizer.

Potash Deficiency. This can potentially happen to all plants and the growth will be slow and younger shoots may appear dull or yellowed. The leaching out of Phosphates is the general cause and happens to soils with high rain fall, heavy clay, and deep peaty soils. You can treat this with Bone meal and Super phosphates.

There are many more reasons why your foliage might not be looking good and I have only scratched the surface with some of these problems you may encounter, and I would encourage seeking further advice if you are still unsure.

Root Problems.

Many problems you may encounter can come from what is happening below the ground or in your compost, so I shall list a few for you to look out for.

Damping Off. Seedlings of all plants can have this problem and the affected roots will darken and rot off causing the plant to die. A variety of fungi cause this, and a fluffy fungal growth can appear on the surface that will quickly spread across the whole tray or pot. There is no effective control once established, so improve ventilation, sow seeds thinly, also improve hygiene and avoid over watering and use only sterilized compost.

Chafer & Cutworms. Cavities will appear in your root crops and can eventually die. You can search for the Cutworm or Larva and dispose of responsible, but if persistent you may need to use a chemical treatment.

Carrot Root Flies. These will appear as rusty brown looking tunnels on the plant roots and the 1 cm long maggot can bore into larger roots and feed under the skin. You can place a two-foot plastic fence to deter the low flying flies from finding the root or in the case of larger attacks a chemical treatment may be required. Companion planting can also be an effective deterrent.

Drought. Unless you have a hose pipe ban, this problem is one of the easiest to avoid and can affect a plants long term growth especially established plant that will be slower to show signs. All plants can be vulnerable, especially pot and container plants and in hot weather will need regular checking for drying out. So, do please check your plants, because prevention is easier that the cure and once a plant has been exposed to chronic water shortage it will be less likely to recover and die.

Black Leg on Cuttings. You will notice that the stem becomes blackened, shrunken, soft, rotten, and normally at the base and then the plant will discolour and die. There are a variety of organisms that cause this which are often spread through unhygienic practices with not cleaning tools, and stagnant water used to water them. The disease can also be transmitted through moist soil. Prevention is easier than the cure so uses cleaned equipment and sterilized compost and you can dip the cuttings in a rooting compound containing a fungicide.

Fungus Gnats. Plants grown under cover are more likely to be affected and seedlings and cutting will fail to grow. Brown Flies will run across the compost and you may see the larva. The white maggots which are about 6 mm in length mainly feed on dead roots but can feed on healthier roots and leaves. The adult flies do not generally cause a problem on healthy plants and sticky fly traps can be hung at surface level to trap the adult flies. You can also help by removing dead leaves and flowers from the surface and by keeping the greenhouse tidy.

Vine weevil Larva. When you have this pest, the plant will grow slowly, wilt, collapse and die. They will gnaw away at the outer tissues of seedlings of woody plants and cuttings from the stems below the soil. The plump white 1 cm long curved Larvae with brown heads can easily be recognised. The adults will lay their eggs in spring and summer and the damage can happen from autumn to spring. Nematodes can be used as a biological treatment, but to my knowledge, no treatment is available to amateur gardeners that will have a lasting effect on older Larva. Good hygiene practices are advised and if persistent to discard potted plants responsibly that are affected, or a chemical treatment may be used on younger Larva.

This is just an overview of the many problems that you might encounter, but please do not worry overly so, because many can easily be solved by detecting early and adhering to a good gardening practice.

PLANTING GUIDES.

In this section I will try to give you an overview on how to propagate your plants with some simple techniques. I guarantee you that whatever soil type, or condition your soil is. There will be a plant for that spot. It can be daunting once you realise how many there are, but it need not be and once you start flicking through those seed catalogues, you will soon see what you like and how best to introduce them into your garden.

You basically have three options when it comes to plants. Grow from seed, propagation or buying the plant. Seeds and propagation are always going to be the cheapest option, unless someone gives you the plant you require, and the most rewarding is always going to be growing your own. What fun is there in just buying the plant when you will by now, I hope, be set up to grow it yourself easily and for a fraction of the cost, and more importantly, be able to grow as many as you like.

The next thing to consider when buying a plant or seed is its life cycle, and this is where reading labels and seed packets is vital. You do not

A GENERAL GUIDE TO FILLING YOUR GARDEN WITH

want to buy a plant that you think is going to flower the first year, an (Annual) then realise you have bought, a (Bi-annual} that lives for two years and produces its flowers in the second year. So do check this when you read the label. Also, when you read a label you may come across the words (hardy) which means they are frost resistant and (half-hardy) which means they are not frost resistant and will need either bringing into a frost-free environment or protecting with horticultural fleece. Another word you will come across is (perennial) and this means any plant living longer than three seasons and generally applies to shrubs and trees, and as your knowledge grows you will want to include these into your collection as a longer term investment to give you garden height and structure. They do take longer to grow, but are well worth it and in the next few pages I shall give you a rough guide on what plants are available along with a good starting point for your home grow vegetables and fruits and some plants that are worth knowing, because that are poisonous. Especially if you have children or pets. You need to beware of the danger they can pose.

Propagating is also a method that is worth considering when increasing your own plants. If you come across a good neighbour's garden, that has established plants and you would like it your own garden. Please do not go and just start hacking at a neighbour or friends' plants, and I am sure if they are keen gardeners, will be more than happy to help and will even show you the best way they know on how to propagate the plant, or give you some seed from it when they are ripe. I shall again give you a rough guide on good plants to do this too, and some simple techniques to try to help you be successful in rooting a cutting.

Annuals. By definition, an annual is a plant that has a life cycle that will last just one season.

Many of you will buy annuals each year and this is probably one of the easiest ways to save money. Firstly, is obviously to buy seed and grow as many as you like. The second is to buy plants early in the season and when you see them being offered in small packs of six, nine or twelve s as young plants. Then you can simply re-pot on in your greenhouse and grow them on before planting out, because as the season goes by, they will be sold in ever-increasing sized pots and become more expensive. Another good way is also to collect seed near the end of the plants flowering season, and instead of pinching out flowering tips to prolong the flowering season. Let a few set seed and collect when ripe, then store in paper bags until next year, and sow as normal. Some species are hybridized and may, revert, back to type, but as they are free. Why not give them a try? Some plants do not lend well to this, but where you can, it is an easy way to have plants for free.

Bi annuals. By definition, are plants that their life cycle lasts for two seasons and generally produce flowers in the second year.

These are almost always going to be a long-term investment, but do not be put off buying these, because money can still be saved by growing on from seed and many can be propagated to increase future supply. Also, many Bi-annuals can be sown early in the year to flower on later like sweet peas so do read labels on planting sowing times, because some Bi-annuals are treated as Annuals. You will pay a bit more for Bi annuals so do look out for end of season bargains that may look unsightly now, but by next year when growth returns. They will soon look at their best once again and as many Bi annuals produce offshoots after the main flowering plant has died these can be carefully taken off and potted on, so do look out for these end of season bargains. If you are going to store these plants in pots over winter, do check them from drying out completely and water sparingly if required and remove dead foliage if storing in a greenhouse as pests & diseases can be harboured, to prevent early outbreaks.

Perennials. By definition, have a life cycle that lasts for more than three seasons.

These plants are a must in any garden as are the others, but where perennials come into their own is providing your garden with structure and when all your annuals have gone past their best with careful selection you can have a perennial in flower virtually all year round. Whether it's a bulb, climber or shrub, they are well worth the investment. It can be trickier to save money with these as the grower has invested a lot more time into them, but savings can be had. If you are extremely patient, then seed growing can be done, but a far better way is cuttings, that I will cover next. End of season bargains is a must, because some plants do die back, and the plant outlet may just want to sell them off to create room for other seasonal plants, so do again, check the bargain sections. Evergreens however you may struggle to get as, they can still look good out of season hence the more reason to have them in your garden as all year-round structure. All plants, especially perennials depend on one thing, and that is you. So do only grow what you can manage comfortably, or you will fill your garden and before long, they will become overgrown and that tranquil haven will soon become a jungle, but with a little knowledge on the plant's needs. It need not be that way so once again, do read labels, because this information will help you, not only choose the right spot, but will help you manage the plants' needs.

Do keep plant labels when buying plants. Firstly, they are a good reference in case you forget something about the plant, and secondly are a ready-made label for you if you choose to grow the plant again or propagate them.

Another tip is to share plants. This is the easiest way to increase yours, your friends and family's stock and from my experience, whether you are just starting out, or a seasoned gardener. We all love talking about them and sharing them, so do not be afraid to ask if you see a plant in their garden you would like to know more about or would like to grow yourself. I am sure they would be more than glad to help you. It would be foolish to think anybody could know everything about gardening, because the subject is vast. So if you do have any problems, just ask at your local garden centre or a knowledgeable gardener, especially when treating pests or diseased looking plants and as I have mentioned before, never apply a chemical treatment unless you are one hundred percent sure you know what you are doing and have read the instructions, and if any doubts, do seek further advice

Seeds. To germinate seeds successfully, you are going to have to provide them with some basic conditions and that is air, moist soil and warmth. Most seeds need a minimum temperature of 10C (50F) to germinate and some considerably higher, so do read the temperature requirements on the label. Sowing times will also need to be considered, because sow too early, unless you provide artificial heat they could fail to germinate, or sow too late, and the plant may not have time during the season to flower, fruit or produce the required crop, again. Do read these guides on the packet or label. Seeds also come in a wide range of sizes and shapes. On a good label it will tell you the depth to sow, but as a good general rule. Plant a seed, two and a half to three times the seed size in depth. A common mistake with smaller seeds is planting too many and as mentioned before, add sand if required for the amount of seed you require and do not be tempted to sow the whole packet, because when they all germinate you will have far too many, and wastage is best avoided and remember it is far better to make two thin sowing s, than one large one. It is also a good idea to not leave germinated seeds too long before pricking out. If you have grown them in a seed tray, as soon as two leaves have emerged you can separate them into individual pots or cells. Try not to damage the plants as the roots can be delicate and are best handled by the leaf after you have teased them out the tray. Provide good air circulation and water sparingly at this early stage to avoid diseases developing.

HERBS.

Herbs are a must for any garden and with a little knowledge can be used in your day to day cooking and can be useful in many ways at not only attracting wildlife, but most of them have the most amazing aromas and if you have a shady area that needs filling, many herbs will be happy to grow there with some preferring it.

ANGELICA. This is a bushy biennial with yellowish, green flowers than can grow to 5-6 feet tall. Sow the first year, then thin to 12 inches apart and will need support, also prefers moist soil & shade.

ANISEED. This is an annual with white dainty flowers and can grow to 12-18 inches tall & may need support in windy areas.

BALM. This is a bushy perennial with white flowers and can grow to 30 inches tall. You can cut this back in the winter and is easily multiplied by root division in spring & prefers moist soil & shade.

BASIL. This is a bushy annual with white flower and can grow 24 inches tall. Thin seeds to 12 inches apart and nip out the tips to encourage bushy growth & likes a rich soil.

BAY. This is an ornamental tree and can grow to 3.5-5 metres tall. You can keep the plant small by pruning, and they do well in containers. It has aromatic leaves and have many uses in cooking.

CHIVES. This is a perennial with round spiky leaves with mauve flowers & will need regular picking and the flowers, removing to keep it vigorous and can be dug up in autumn and the bulbs divided to increase your plants.

CORIANDER. This is an annual with pink lacy flowers that can grow to 24 inches tall. Has many uses in cooking.

DILL. This is an annual with bluish green feathery leaves and can grow to 36 inches tall. Thin seedlings to 12-15 inches apart. Will need shelter and support.

MINT. This is a perennial with purple flowers and can grow to 24-36 inches tall. They can be propagated from root decision and are best grown in sunken pots or in containers, because of their invasive nature. There are many varieties on offer, including apple mint, peppermint & pineapple mint.

PARSLEY. This is a biennial, perennial & has greenish yellow flowers & can grow to 12 -24 inches tall. It also likes shade in the summer and the sun in the winter & prefers rich soils, also can be very slow to germinate.

ROSEMARY. This is grown as a perennial shrub and can grow to 1.5 – 2 metres tall and has mauve flowers. It is best grown from cuttings and likes lime soils.

SAGE. This is a bushy perennial with violet flowers and can grow to 24 inches tall. It is best replaced every three years.

TARRAGON. This is a bushy perennial with tiny greenish white flowers and can grow to 12 -18 inches tall. It can be propagated from root division and is best replaced every three to four years also likes poorer soils.

THYME. This is a bushy perennial with mauve flowers and can grow to 12 inches tall. They are best propagated by root division and replaced every three to four years, and they like lime soils and there are many other varieties.

These are just a few common herbs I have mentioned and there are plenty more, and well worth a place in any garden.

HAZARDOUS & POISONOUS PLANTS.

If you are going to start propagating your plants, it is always best to know the poisonous ones. So, I thought it would be prudent to introduce you to a few of the more common species you should be careful with, because some can be bought, and others may be growing in your garden already.

Poisonous Flowering Plants.

MONKS HEAD. All parts of the plant & said by many to be the most dangerous.
AUTUMN CROCUS MEADOW SAFFRON. All parts of the plant particularly corms & seeds.
LILY OF THE VALLEY. All parts of the plant.
LARKSPUR. Seeds & foliage.
FOXGLOVE. All parts of the plant.
CHRISTMAS ROSE BLACK HELLEBORE. All parts of the plant.
IRIS BLUE FLAG. Possibly all parts.
LUPIN'S. All parts, especially the seeds.
NARCISSUS DAFFODIL JONQUIL. Bulb.

A GENERAL GUIDE TO FILLING YOUR GARDEN WITH

AMERICAN MANDRAKE. All parts, especially green unripe berries.

Poisonous Garden Vegetable Plants.

RHUBARB. Leaves, but not stalks which are edible.
POTATO. Green sprouting tubers, stems, & leaves.

Poisonous Ornamental Shrubs & Trees.

BROOM. Seeds
LABURNUM GOLDEN RAIN. All parts, particularly bark & seeds.
CHERRY LAUREL. All parts, particularly leaves & fruit kernels.
RHODODENDRON, AZALEA, AMERICAN LAUREL, CALICO BUSH, SHEEP LAUREL, MOUNTAIN LAUREL. The leaves and flowers.
YEW. The leaves & seeds, the latter are deadly and the red pulp covering the seed is the least harmful.

Poisonous Weeds & Hedgerow Plants.

DEADLY NIGHT SHADE. All parts.
WHITE BRYONY. Roots & berries.
GREATER CELANDINE. All parts, particularly the roots.
THORN APPLE. The leaves, unripe capsules & especially the seeds.
SPURGE. All parts.
PRIVET. Berries & possibly the leaves.
BUTTERCUPS & CROWS FOOTS. The sap.
WOODY NIGHTSHADE, BITTERSWEET. All parts.
BLACK NIGHT SHADE, GARDEN NIGHTSHADE. All

parts.
BLACK BRYONY. The roots & berries.

Poisonous Woodland Plants.

FLY AGARIC, PANTHER CAP, DEATH CAP MUSH-ROOMS- All parts.
CUCKOO PINT. All parts, especially the berries.
SPURGE LAUREL. All parts, particularly the bark & berries.
DOGS MERCURY. All parts.
OAK. Acorns & leaves.
POISON IVY. All parts.

Boggy Areas or Swamp Plants.

MARSH MARIGOLD, KING CUP. Sap.
COW BANE. The roots, leaves & flowers.
HEMLOCK. All parts, especially young leaves & unripe fruit.
HEMLOCK, WATER DROP-WORT. All parts, especially the roots.

Poisonous House Plants.

DUMB CANE. All parts.
POINSETTIA. Juice of the stem, leaves, flower & fruit.
HYACINTH. The Bulb.
CASTER OIL PLANT. The seeds.
MISTLETOE. The berries.

I have just included the common plants names and a lot of them you would not normally grow,

A GENERAL GUIDE TO FILLING YOUR GARDEN WITH

but you need to be aware of. Especially those of you with children and pets, so do be careful if you come across any of these, because there are many more and if you believe you, your children or pets have encounter any of them. Then seek medical advice straight away and if safe to do so, take a sample of the plant, taking precautions when handling it, or take a picture. We almost, all, have camera phones now and if you do need medical assistance it will help to recognise the plant and aid in diagnosis and treatment. Some botanical, or Latin names may have been updated, but the common names rarely are, so do read labels carefully and take the necessary precautions.

VEGETABLES & FRUIT.

Vegetables and fruits are always fun to have in any garden and when you see the delight on your children or grand children's faces when they eat a fresh pea out of the pod, or a fresh strawberry straight from the plant you will see why, but they can also be a useful seasonal staple and can save you money so do add these where you can, and many are simple to grow. Firstly, you might be tempted to grow far too many and be over ambitious and this is where your time is important, because you only should grow what you can comfortably look after. Plants need looking after so do keep this in mind when you go out and buy them. Secondly, and probably the most important is only growing what you like to eat, and this will apply when space is limited. Growing from seed is always going to be the cheapest option and with a packet of seed you can in many instances use this again next year and thus saving again on cost. If you have an allotment size plot you wish to fill then you are going to need to put a three-year crop rotation plan in place to prevent the build-up of disease and make a more detailed plan of what you want to grow, this requires me to write a separate book on the subject, because it requires a lot more detail than I can give you in this guide, but for our purposes we are using the addition of vegetables and fruit to complement your garden and not produce them on an allotment scale.

There are many worth adding to your garden that can be simply added to a space in the border or grown on in the cold frame and greenhouse. If you do want to grow them primarily in the greenhouse, then summer shading will be needed. Tomatoes will normally be fine without shading, but Cucumbers will not, so a little consideration will be needed when choosing plants for this environment and early in the year they may seem fine, but as the weather heats up they will suffer heat exhaustion, so again do read plant label requirements. Another good tip is to look out for those long plastic troughs. I have acquired several at my local reuse centre for pennies but are generally not to expensive brand-new. These are ideal for growing carrots, spring onions, radishes, lettuce, etc. and you can simply sow a row of them in the greenhouse or cold frame and can be useful in protecting your crop from pests especially slug & snails and as the season warms up simple move them outdoors to finish growing. Do be careful when picking these trays up as they can be heavy and is best that you get the help from a friend to lift them.

BEANS. These can be some of the easiest to accommodate in your garden and require little space. Sow directly into the ground or in pots for planting out later. Support will be needed. There are many varieties on offer so do be adventurous and not only consider runner beans. They are greedy feeders so do add plenty of organic matter before planting.

BEETROOT. These can be germinated easily and are worth considering for their vibrant leaves but will run to seed if left without watering and in poor soil.

CARROTS. There are so many excellent varieties on offer and I prefer to grow these in the long plastic trays, because I can provide a better growing medium for them and keep a better eye out for root flies which can ruin a crop. Simple to grow and successive crops can be sown and harvested through the season.

CUCUMBERS & COURGETTES. Definitely worth growing and make sure plants are watered well through the season and fed with a tomato fertilizer once the fruits have set. Harvest regularly, for successful crops. There are many varieties indoor and out and given the right conditions, can grow rapidly so do take this into account if space is limited.

LETTUCE. There are plenty of varieties on offer

so be adventurous. Good, moist, fertile soil conditions is required and water liberally in dry conditions, or they will tend to bolt and run to seed.

SPRING ONIONS. A great crop to have but can be slow to germinate. Again, I prefer to grow these in rows in long plastic trays and sown at intervals to avoid a glut and you can have fresh crops throughout the growing season.

RADISHES. A fun crop to grow and one of the simplest and fastest. Successive sowing is recommended and again I prefer to grow them in long plastic troughs. Slugs and Snails love to eat them so do check regularly. Many varieties on offer with milder flavours.

TOMATOES. These can be simple to grow when following some simple rules. Germination can be slow if you have not provided a minimum temperature so do read the label. Trailing or bush varieties plants will need tips removed to encourage side shoots and upright or cordon varieties will freely put outside shoots so remove these carefully as they grow, conserving the plant's energy on growing tomatoes and not unneeded plant material. Pinch out the growing tip once four or five truces have set, because it will be difficult for the plant to ripen any more than this in one season and you want to concentrate its energies on the tomatoes you have. Begin feeding as soon as a plant has set the first fruit.

PEPPERS. A great plant to have in the greenhouse and many varieties to choose from indoors and out. They are best grown as pot plants and you can keep a better eye on them for insects that like to eat the fruits. Again, liquid tomato fertilizer to be used once fruit has formed and with the many colours and varieties on offer are well worth having for their decorative appeal.

This is just a general overview of some staple plants to grow in conjunction with your others, but there are many more worth considering depending on what space you have available, because some do need larger areas, so do read labels on height and spread.

Fruits come under two main categories, soft and hard fruits. This is where space is going to be a factor for growing them, but if you like growing plants in containers it is possible to grow many soft & hard fruits in them. Seasonal soft fruits can be expensive, so if you can, it is well worth adding them to your collection.

STRAWBERRIES. In essence, you only have to buy a strawberry plant once and you should never have to buy another, because they set runners out freely through the growing season and can be easily rooted on to make a new plant to replace your stock plants every two to three years to keep your stock healthy and vigorous. The main pest you will see is the damage left by slugs & snails after they have sampled the fruits. You can deter these by putting straw around the plant.

GOOSEBERRIES. These can be an acquired taste, but are easy to grow, forming dense spiny bushes so prune regularly following the pruning recommendation when buying. There are many varieties on offer.

RASPBERRIES. These can be bought as bare rooted or pot grown. You will need to find out whether they are late or early cropping as both have different pruning requirements.

These are just my three favourite soft fruits to grow, but there are many more and with just some careful planning, soil conditioning and pruning, can be very rewarding, but do be warned. Many birds and pests like them also, so do not always expect to eat them first and you may need to provide protection against attacks. Some other soft fruits to consider are Blackberries, Currents and Blueberries, but do read the labels and pruning recommendations and if space is limited, again only select what you want to eat.

Hard fruits are going to cost you more money, simply because the grower has had to spend time and effort in raising the plants and rightly so, should be more expensive. These are a long-term investment and should only be bought if you intend to look after them carefully. You can save money by buying bare rooted plants but do be warned to look out for healthy specimens that are still dormant and are not showing signs of growth, because they may already be under stress and may or may not recover. Also, do check height and spread, because in years to come many can grow rapidly and take over a site if not pruned correctly or neglected. A good option if you want to grow these types are on grafted root stocks, this is basically a variety that has been grafted onto a less vigorous root system. They can be container grown and with some simple pruning can be productive for years, but you will pay a premium, but as this book is about saving you money unless you have it within your budget you probably will not buy them and again with the cost involved, if you do buy these, do look after them and read the instruction on caring for them.

CUTTINGS.

Cuttings can be a useful way to increase your stock plants and can be categorized into different seasonal growth stages as listed below.

SOFT WOOD CUTTINGS. These are generally taken in spring from a parent plant from growing material that is almost mature and beginning to harden. They are taken from the growing tips and can also be taken from herbaceous perennial basal shoots. They do need a supportive environment as they can wilt as they lose water quickly but are generally the best way to root a cutting. Take the cutting from below a node and plant in a free draining gritty compost mixture. A hormone rooting powder can be used to help speed up rooting and prevent infections.

Some worth trying are:

DAHLIAS. Taken between February to March
DELPHINIUM. Taken between February to March
DIANTHUS. Taken from non-flowering shoots in summer.
FUCHSIA. Taken from non-flowering shoots in June

HYDRANGEA. Taken in May to June
PENSTEMON. Taken in summer

GREENWOOD CUTTINGS. These are similar to softwood cutting and can be taken from early to mid-summer and generally survive better but may take longer to root and will still require a supportive environment. Take cutting as you would a softwood cutting.

SEMI RIPE CUTTING. These can be taken in late summer and are less prone to wilting, because the tissue is slightly firmer and prepare as you would a softwood cutting and, in some cases, can be taken as you would Hardwood cuttings.
Some worth trying are;
CAMELLIA. Taken in June to July
CEANOTHUS. Taken in July to August
POTENTILLA. Taken in June to July
RHODODENDRON. Taken in July

HARDWOOD CUTTINGS. These can be taken from fully mature wood and are generally taken towards the end of a plant growing season in autumn and through to the spring when the tissue is fully ripe. They are the easiest to look after but can be slow to root. They are the largest cutting to be taken, because they need the food reserves inside the tissue to root. Many climbers and roses do well with this method. When taking the cutting it should be above and below a leaf nod and about around 2-5 inches in length, allowing for five or

six nods between and all the leaves removed. It is also a good idea using a sharp knife to make an angular cut at the base to reveal the cadmium layer and increasing the chances of rooting. These can be then planted to a depth just below the node.
Some worth trying are;
BUDDLEIA. Taken in October to November
CORNUS. Taken in October to November
ILEX. Taken in October to November in a cold frame
ROSES. Taken in October to November

Cuttings with leafy material left on can be better cared for by covering them with a plastic bag to retain a high humidity and if necessary, place a frame inside the bag to prevent the cuttings touching the plastic as this can cause them to rot. If you can provide bottom heat in a propagator, then this can speed up root development. Once you see new growth appearing, you can then pot the cuttings on. For the more adventurous leaf cuttings can be tried and root cuttings, but these are sadly being used less. There are many ways to propagate plants and these are just a few basic methods but do try others and see what works for you.

COLD FRAME AS A NURSERY.

Traditionally, a cold frame is used for hardening off plants ready to be planted out and protecting them over the winter. However, if you do not have the space for a greenhouse your cold frame will come in very handy as an alternative and although not ideal it will help you to raise your plants and ensure a better success rate, because in the early part of the year a late frost can wipe out all your hard work so protecting plants that cannot withstand frost is going to be vital. Construct your cold frame as large as you possibly can, because you will fill it in no time at all. Make it so it has a sloping top and for our purposes in a bright and sunny location and on those warm spring days do remember to keep the lid open and regularly check your plants for drying out. If you can accommodate both a greenhouse and cold frame then fantastic, because they are perfect for hardening off plants ready to plant out and will save you time each day from having to bring them back into the greenhouse and at this busy time of the

A GENERAL GUIDE TO FILLING YOUR GARDEN WITH

year space is always at a premium.

Germination time for a plant is going to be for you the most critical, because all plants like different temperatures and some will not grow until this is just right, again read the label for optimum lows and highs for a better success and also the time of year to sow. A good way for you to do this is to put them on a sunny window sill, but again, do check regularly for drying out, because a newly germinated seed needs your help to survive and only you can provide all it needs at this stage, so do check and water sparingly. Little and open is better at this stage than soaking the plants and letting them sit in soggy compost and will only encourage disease so vigilance is key. It takes seconds to do and as the plants are in your home, you can do this easily. Once they are looking like they are growing strong and the weather hopefully improving then move them on to the cold frame and once your windowsill has more room, then repeat this process again. As the weather warms up you can put your sown seeds directly into the cold frame to germinate. A word of warning, do check your cold frame for slugs and snails daily, if possible, and lift up pots to see if any are hiding, because in one sitting, a hungry slug or snail can munch through a whole tray or pot of your delicious seedlings, and they will find them. You can if you wish, put slug pellets in the cold frame, but do be aware they are there and remove any killed slugs or snails to keep your cold frame clean and remember this is a nursery not a storage facility, because pests will hide in there and delight on your plants when you're not looking. Hygiene is paramount to your success and not only will it save you the disappointment of losing your plants it will save you money on not having to buy pest controls, so do keep both your greenhouse and cold frame free from unnecessary clutter and litter and wash all used pots to prevent the spread of pests and disease.

I have just given you a general idea on how a cold frame can be used to raise your plants through the year and you can then adapt this, to what you want to grow and that is the next tip. It is always tempting when you first start out to go wild and take on too much. I have done this many time, and still do. Your success is going to be down to one thing, and that is time. Only raise and grow what you can comfortably look after and do not fall into the trap of being over ambitious, because once you build a collection of plants. They need looking after, and neglect will kill them as quickly and I do not want you to lose heart and struggle to manage when starting out, because it will deflate you and put you off. So, whether you are an experienced gardener or just beginning, only take on what you can comfortably look after and this way, it remains enjoyable and not a burden that you feel tied to. I am not aiming to laden your life with an endless task of plant management, but merely enhancing your life with the joy of raising plants at a low cost, so do take this into account when buying and propagating them.

FERTILISERS & USES.

At some point all good soils can suffer an imbalance in nutrients and with experience, you will be able to diagnose some of these by looking at the tell-tail signs that a plant is displaying. There are many on the market to choose from, so I shall just give you an overview of the commonly used types but do read the labels carefully if you are unsure how to apply them and do seek professional advice first.

NITROGEN. Soils that are susceptible are acid, wet, thin and sandy soils.

Dried Blood (organic) is quick acting, especially in warm moist soils and can be top dressed throughout the growing season.
Hoof and Horn meal (organic) acts fairly quickly in warm soils and is long-lasting and can be top dressed throughout the growing season.
Nitrate of Soda (inorganic) is soluble and acts immediately when watered in and can be top dressed in the spring or summer.
Nitro Chalk (inorganic) the chalk content balances out any lime loss caused by any ammonia

that is present and can be applied in spring or summer.

Potash nitrate (inorganic) Acts Quickly and supplies Potash as well as Nitrogen and can be top dressed in spring or summer.

Sulphate of Ammonia (inorganic) is quick acting in warm soils, but repeated use may make some soils to acid, but are good for chalky soils. It can be applied directly to the soil or diluted as a liquid feed in spring or summer, but do not mix with lime.

PHOSPHOROUS (phosphates). Very wet or acid soils can be susceptible to deficiencies and some peaty soils.

Bone Meal (organic) releases phosphates slowly over a long period and the nitrogen content acts quickly. This should be dug in during the autumn and winter before sowing or planting.

Basic Slag (inorganic) is slow acting and long-lasting. This should be dug in at autumn or winter before sowing and planting and should not be used with lime.

Super phosphate of Lime (inorganic) acts quickly and is good for root crops and seedbeds and does not supply lime and can be used at any time before sowing.

POTASSIUM (potash). Light, chalky and very sandy soils can be affected by this deficiency and poorly drained soils.

Potash Nitrate (inorganic) acts quickly and can supply Nitrogen as well and is best used as a top dressing in spring or summer.

Sulphate of Potash (inorganic) acts quickly and is held in by clay and humus and can be raked in before sowing and planting.

There however, some other deficiencies other than the main three I have mentioned that can occur and I shall give you a quick overview of these, but again if you are in any doubt seeking professional advice.

CALCIUM (lime). This generally can occur in strongly acid soils and can be redressed with Sulphate of Potash, Potash of Lime or Lime and is applied before planting.

MAGNESIUM. Deficiency can occur in wet areas or in seasons with large rain fall, sandy soils, soils that have been over manured with Potash fertilizers and can normally be redressed with Magnesium Sulphate (Epsom salts) or Magnesium Limestone. You can apply to the soil or spray over the leaves.

BORON. Deficiency can occur on limey or over limed soils and can be redressed with Iron chelate and mixed into the soil before planting.

IRON. Deficiency can occur on very limey or over limed soils and can be redressed with Borax (sodium tetraborate) and is sprayed on the leaves and are applied to the soil.

MANGANESE. Deficiency can occur on very limey or over limed soils or in many peaty soils and is treated with Manganese Sulphate and sprayed onto the leaves.

COPPER. Deficiency can occur on some peaty soils and sandy reclaimed heath land and can be treated by applying Copper Sulphate onto the soil before sowing or planting.

MOLYBDENUM. Deficiency can occur in very acid soils and is usually cured by Liming, but molybdenum may be applied before sowing and planting.

There are some good sources of Organic fertilizers around ranging from Animal Manure, Garden compost, Bone meal, Fish blood & Bone, Hoof & Horn, Seaweed Meal, Mushroom compost, Rock potash, Wood ash, Pelleted chicken manure and Cocoa shells, so do experiment with those that are within your price ranges and see what works best in your garden.

Some good inorganic fertilizers worth considering also are Growing more, Ammonium Nitrate, Triple super phosphate, Potassium chloride and Potassium Sulphate all of which will come under their own brand names.

FROM THE AUTHOR.

There is no doubt in my mind that the Planet is changing. Our modern lifestyles don't always give us everything we need to stay fit and healthy. Technology has given us so much but has also taken away from us just as much. It is a proven fact that gardening has so many health benefits to you, and your family and it is mostly free. A worrying trend is that new housing developments have increasingly smaller gardens. This not only adds pressure on our wildlife by creating less diverse habitats, but also dilutes our need to maintain our outdoor spaces with even less to do. A small garden can still be a haven for wildlife and can still be enjoyed, but this is where as gardeners we do need to become more aware that for our wildlife to thrive in our gardens, more needs to be done by us to create those habitats that are less abundant in a larger garden. If you have taken anything from this book, I hope that it is to be more proactive in your garden, and wherever you can, do please encourage wildlife into your garden, because sadly. Once it is gone, it is gone forever!

A GENERAL GUIDE TO FILLING YOUR GARDEN WITH

The following section is a month by month guide to show you what, and when to do you planting and some extra tips to help you through the gardener's year.

JANUARY.

January can seem a long, cold, drawn out month with its frosty mornings and short days, but there are jobs that could be done this month. Christmas and the new year have passed, and the shortest day is well behind us now. It's time to start thinking about the gardening year ahead of us. It is also a great time of year to start making plans for the garden. At this time of year your garden will look at barest, the trees are naked, many of the border plants have died off and sleeping out the winter, but there are glimmers of life emerging from the soil. Soon, Springtime flowers will be showing the first signs of growth through the soil and will be coming into their own. Snow drops are the first sign for me that Spring is finally coming and those beautiful white clumps of flowers a welcoming sight. There is a surprising amount of colour to be had at this time of year and with the right choice of plants you could have some welcoming colour in your borders.

The winter weather can be unpredictable at this time of year and yield some severe frosts and snow, so those few remaining jobs may need to be put on hold until the weather breaks and allows you to get back out there.

As I mentioned early, now is a good time to plan ahead. If there is a part of your garden that hasn't quite performed as you wanted, or the plants you had in a border didn't quite meet your expectations, then now is a good time to start thinking about how to make those changes. Or you may just fancy redeveloping part of the garden, a new pond feature or patio. Whatever the change you are thinking about, this is the embryonic stages of that change or makeover. At this stage jot down the ideas, plan them on a piece of paper and try to visualise them in your garden. Later on, in the year when the weather allows you too, start introducing those changes.

It is also a great time of year to start looking at those plant catalogues and start planning which new plants you would like to introduce into your garden.

FLOWERS.

-If you have lifted and potted up half-hardy perennials and put them under cover or in the greenhouse, they will need extra protection this month during prolonged spells of cold.

-Herbaceous plants left in the ground may need protecting, so if you are unsure if they are hardy then mulch around roots, paying particular attention to cover round crowns.

- Now is a good time to go through seeds catalogues and decide on what plants you intend to grow this year.

- Hardy plants to sow in the greenhouse are Pansies, Antirrhinums, Violas, Cornflowers

- Roses can be tied up and any leggy stems reduced by half to prevent wind damage in readiness for pruning in March. Collect any leaves under rose bushes to prevent black-spot overwintering.

- Summer annuals like Pelargoniums, Sweat Peas, and Begonias can be sown now. A heated propagator or sunny windowsill will be required for germination.

- Heathers are in season right now so to ensure success, plant deeply adding plenty of organic material and a dusting of bone meal. Trim spent flowers regularly to promote bushy growth.

- If you intend to plant climbers next to a wall, the soil here can be barren. Ideally dig to a two-spade depth and add plenty of organic material.

- Fuchsias that have been potted up and rested over winter can now be started into growth at the end of this month. Clean off any dead material and prune back to 1-2 inches long. Bring into a warm place and water lightly. When new growth begins re-pot into fresh compost and move into a cooler light area to promote strong, firm, short jointed growth.

VEGETABLES.

- If you are looking to grow a large Onion variety,

now is the time to plant them.

-Shallots can be planted for an early alternative to spring onions.

-Early varieties of Potatoes can be potted up in a light, frost free place and brought on early to enjoy a crop a few weeks earlier than outdoor grown plants. Also, order seed Potatoes now for planting out in March.

-Many crops are still in season such as Beetroot, Brussels sprouts, Cabbage, Carrots, Onions, Parsnips, Potatoes and Shallots, and Pigeons can cause a lot of damage to winter greens. Cover with mesh or netting to prevent damage.

-Early hardy Pea and Broad bean sown now will need protecting from prolonged cold spells with cloches.

-If you have stored vegetables, check regularly for rot and disease, dispose of to prevent it spreading to other crops.

-Cabbage roots should be cleared away straight after harvest to prevent harbouring pests and disease which could infect crops later on in the year.

-Now is good time, if you have not already done so to dig over and manure your vegetable plot in preparation for planting time.

-Parsnip beds can be prepared now. Dig over, removing large stones and dig in fine organic material to prevent roots forking.

-Rhubarb will benefit from a thick layer of well-rotted manure. If you want to force some young tender shoots, then place a large terracotta pot over the crown.

FRUIT.

-Now is a good time to apply a Tar wash to your fruit trees to protect them against overwintering disease spores and kill off pests. Pay attention to all the nooks and crannies that may harbour pests and disease.

-If you have fruit cages, remove netting to prevent it being damaged by heavy snow.

-Autumn fruiting Raspberries can be pruned to ground level.

-Red and white currants can be pruned now. Cut back the main shoots to about 3 inches of new growth, shortening side shoots to a single bud.

-Peach trees can have a copper fungicide applied now and protect them against rain splash in Winter to prevent peach leaf curl disease.

-Pot grown plants can be brought into the greenhouse now to encourage early crops.

-Vines can be pruned. Shorten side shoots to 1 or 2 buds from the main stem.

-Protect Gooseberries and Currents with netting to prevent birds stripping off the new buds.

-Blueberries will benefit from a generous mulch of high acidity compost.

-Cherry trees can be difficult to protect fruit on large specimens. By selecting a tree that has been grafted on a dwarf root stock can be easily protected with netting to protect fruit. Do check you have selected a self-fertile variety, but if you plan to plant more than one then the choice of varieties is greatly increased.

-Continue planting fruit trees and bushes.

TREES & SHRUBS.

-Deciduous trees and shrubs can be pruned now when weather permits this to be done, they can also be planted out into their permanent position when weather permits.

-Heavy snow should be knocked of evergreens to prevent damage.

-Trees and shrubs can be planted out now. Prepare the ground well and dig deeply mixing in fertiliser and if the soil is in a poor condition add compost. If conditions are very wet and cold it will be better to wait until the weather improves. Try to complete all bare rooted trees, shrubs and roses by March, before the plants come back into growth.

-Check newly planted trees and shrubs after hard frosts and heel in if necessary, to firm the ground around the root ball.

-Before growth begins, Pollarded trees can be pruned to keep them within manageable size.

-If rabbits are a problem, protect new trees with wire mesh or trunk bands to prevent lower bark being chewed off.

BULBS.

-Keep a check on pot grown bulbs and do not allow them to become waterlogged or too dry.

Protection will be needed during long spells of cold weather.

-Lilies can be potted up now to be planted out later when the weather improves.

-At this time of year many outlets will be selling bulbs cheaply to clear stocks, so if you did not manage to buy and plant them out in the Autumn, there is still time to grab a bargain and pot them on in the greenhouse to be planted out later on.

-Snowdrops will be in flower this month and can also be lifted and divided in spells of milder weather.

-If you are looking for colour in your garden at this time of year there is a surprising amount to choose from and none easier to grow than from bulbs. Aconite, Cyclamen, Anemones, Crocus, Iris and Narcissus have all early varieties to choose from and are a welcome early splash of colour.

THE GREENHOUSE.

-If you have not already, your greenhouse would benefit from a good clean down. It is surprising how much light algae on the glass can prevent good quality light from entering. With soapy warm water and a squeegee on a nice day, it is a satisfying job to do and will benefit you later on when you start sowing again. It also a good time to clean all those used pots and have a general tidy up to prevent overwintering pests building up and feasting on any plants you intend to grow on later in the spring.

-Conserve heat in the greenhouse by lining the inside with bubble wrap.

-Cold frames will also benefit from a clean and general tidy ensuring the glass is clean and the lid is fully working.

-Overwintering Alpines will need good ventilation in the greenhouse, weather permitting, but do keep out damp air.

-Now is a good time to ensure heaters and propagators are working correctly.

-Clear snow off greenhouses and cold frames to improve light levels.

-When weather permits, ventilate the greenhouse to ensure a good supply of air is circulated to prevent the build-up of harmful moulds which can rot stems and leaves.

-Water plants sparingly in the morning to allow plants to dry out before night-time frost can harm your plants. A spray bottle is ideal for this to help prevent overwatering. If you do overwater a plant, tap out of the pot and leave to dry out. Repot as soon as the plant begins to dry out.

-Ensure all maintenance of greenhouse is done and replace broken panes of glass if necessary.

-If you have potted up Chrysanthemums, once flowering is finished cut back to 12 inches from the base.

THE POND.

-Ice is the problem to keep an eye out for this month. Use a pan of hot water placed on the ice to melt a breath hole for fish. Frogs can also overwinter in ponds and also will need to breath. Do not be tempted to break the ice because the shock wave could startle fish and kill them.

-Herons can be a welcome visitor to your garden, but they will be looking for lunch. Where you can prevent losses, is by placing a terracotta ridge tile, or pipe into the pond to give your fish a hiding place.

-If snow falls during spells on your pond when being frozen, this can prevent light getting through. Clear off snow as soon as possible.

THE ROCK GARDEN.

-At this time of year your Alpines will benefit from a top dressing of gravel or shingle to help protect them from severe wet weather.

-Waterlogged sites are the most probable cause of Alpines failing at this time of year. Alpines grow best in sunny free draining soil with their roots moist but not wet. To redress this problem, dig in gravel or shingle to improve drainage. If your Alpine bed is extremely waterlogged, then it will be better to redo the whole bed and start from scratch. Clear out the bed completely. Dig out a spades depth and retain the soil. Then dig over this bottom layer adding plenty of gravel, shingle or grit. Replace the top layer added liberal amounts of gravel, shingle or grit. Replace your decorative stone or rocks paying attention to the strata lines within sedimentary rocks to give a natural look to the positioning of the stones to emulate Alpine plants natural habitat. Try to aim for these strata lines within the rocks to run parallel. Divide plants if necessary, at this stage to increase stocks. Reposition your Alpines in an eye pleasing display, then replant. Top dress the soil with a decorative gravel or shingle. Choosing a similar gravel or shingle to the rocks you have will give a more natural look to the bed and show off your Alpines better. Before you start this work to save you time on a big clean up, lay out a large tarpaulin and place all your Stones, soil and plants on this as you clear out the bed. Use another tarpaulin for your topsoil if required. This not only allows you to see clearly what materials you have, and how best to replace them, it also protects the area where you intend to place these materials and will prevent a large unsightly mess after you redo the bed.

LAWN CARE.

-In heavy spells of snow try to avoid piling this onto your lawn as this can damage the lawn underneath.

-If you are planning a new lawn in the Spring, now is a good time to prepare the ground, and allow time for the soil to settle before laying or seeding the new lawn.

-Avoid walking on the lawn during spells of heavy frost.

-During heavy spells of rain you may find areas of

your lawn that are waterlogged, make a note of these areas and correct later in the year by either air-rating by spiking the area, or if the area is seriously waterlogged, then a drainage system may need to be implemented.

-If you have not already done so, on those dry days rake up the remaining leaves that have fallen. Your lawns will also be looking not at their best and it could be tempting to bring the lawn mower out on a nice day, this is definitely not a good idea. The frosts will damage the grass and make it look worse.

-Areas where you intent to sow early crops will benefit from being covered with polythene or an old carpet to help warm the soil in readiness later on.

-Weather permitting, your borders can be tidied up now. Clear leaves and twigs then lightly fork over the area.

-The compost heap will benefit from being turned over now. Dig thoroughly, incorporating the different layers and breaking up any clumped together material. Cover with polythene or an old carpet to continue decomposing.

-This month can be particularly harsh for wildlife with prolonged spells of the garden being frozen solid. Birds will not be able to forage easily, and hibernating insects can be killed off by the cold. With the masses of research going on, there is no doubt many species are struggling to survive and

A GENERAL GUIDE TO FILLING YOUR GARDEN WITH

your garden is becoming more important in trying to preserve the wildlife we have. It is difficult to predict the future of many species now under stress by their habitats declining, chemicals we have been using in our environment and global warming starting to make its real effects known. As gardeners, we can do many things to help. Listed below are some pointers on what you can do this month to help. I shall also give you each month some wildlife to look out for, along with the things we can do, not only to attract more wildlife into our gardens, but also the plants you can plant to benefit them through the year.

-Check bird feeders and tables daily and remove frozen water from bird baths. A good tip for saving cost on bird seed is to buy larger sacks of seed. This with work out cheaper than buying smaller bags and will ensure you have a plentiful supply because you will be surprised at how much seed will consumed at this time of year, especially during prolong spells of cold weather.

-When doing your garden clean up, spare a thought for earthworms. They consume many fallen leaves during the Winter so try not to be over rigorous in collecting every single leaf that has fallen.

-Moss in your lawn may be unsightly, but where you can, leave an area untouched and when you look out into your garden in the early morning you will see why. Many bird's species forage through the moss for insects and some collect it

for nesting.
-If you have amassed a large amount of material during the winter to burn off now, move all the material to check to see if hedgehogs have used the area to hibernate inside.

FEBRUARY.

This month can be tricky in the garden and the days are noticeably getting longer and on sunny days you can feel more heat from the sun. The weather can play some terrible tricks on us and suddenly Spring can feel like it has arrived early, and Winter may seem it has passed. You may be tempted to start mowing the lawn or planting out early varieties of plants as the nights have been unusually mild. Winter can return with vengeance and undo all you hard work and no more so than with tender seedlings that have been brought into the cold greenhouse from your windowsill or propagator, because the daytime temperatures have hit double figures in there. Tempting as it may be, don't try to beat the weather and race ahead of the gardening calendar, nature always wins and will save you the disappointment of trays of dead seedlings or a lawn that has been mowed to short and the frosts and snow have returned.

FLOWERS.

-Summer annuals like Ageratum, Antirrhinum, Begonia, Impatiens Marigolds, Nasturtium, Pelargonium, Petunias, sweat Peas and Zinnia can be sown in a heated propagator or sunny windowsill.

-Continue to water Fuchsias and Pelargoniums kept over winter. Prune Fuchsias, and re-pot to stimulate growth. Check for overwintering pests.

-Prepare beds ready for Sweat peas raised in the Autumn.

-Tidy Winter bedding plants, Violas, Wallflowers and Pansies. Dead head spent blooms and remove yellowing foliage.

-Wisterias need pruning twice a year to promote flowering. All side shoots pruned last summer will need to be reduced further, leaving just two buds. Check ties and replace any that are broken, also add new ties for further training in leaders.

-Sow Sweat Peas now if you want them to flower in June. Soak for 24 hours then sow as normal.

-Chrysanthemum cuttings can be taken now once new side shoots of last year's stools have grown to 3 inches. Strip of the bottoms leaves and cut below a joint. Dip in hormone powder and insert to one third their length into gritty compost and water well. Place in heated propagator, and they should root in about two to three weeks' time.

-Start planning your herbaceous borders. These need a little more thought, because the plants will be in the same position for a few years and will prevent planting errors later on. These are best planted up in Spring, so look through seed cata-

A GENERAL GUIDE TO FILLING YOUR GARDEN WITH

logues for inspiration if you are unsure of what to plant.

VEGETABLES.

-Now is a good time to clear away old winter crops and dig over vacant patches in preparation for new plants.

-If you have not already done so, order seed Potatoes, Onions and Shallots.

-Seed orders should be placed by now and make a sowing time plan from the seed packet instructions. Pay particular attention to sowing times and temperatures required for a better germination success rate.

-Continue to sow hardy Peas and Broad beans under cloches.

-Garlic can now be planted outside.

-Start to chit Potato seed.

-Continue to cover ground with cloches and polythene for early seed sowing.

-Many crops are still in season such as Broccoli, Brussels sprouts, Cabbage, Carrots, Onions, Leeks Parsnips, Potatoes, Shallots, Swedes and Pigeons can cause a lot of damage to winter greens. Cover with mesh or netting to prevent damage.

-Rhubarb that needs to be divided can be dug up now and replanted in a manure enriched soil. Ensure each divided section has a crown and roots.

FRUIT.

-Apples and Pears can be pruned to control vigour

and shape

-Gooseberries can be pruned now. Cut out overcrowded and crossed branches, and older wood, to let in air and light. Reduced shoots to 3 inches and cover with netting to prevent bird damaging buds.

-Raspberries that fruited in the Autumn can still be pruned this month. Prune to ground level. Mulch with well-rotted manure and apply a general fertiliser.

-Strawberries grown outside can be covered with cloches to give an early crop.

-Fertilise around fruit trees with sulphate of potash.

-Give fruit trees a Tar wash to control disease and kill overwintering pests.

-Spray Peach trees with copper fungicide to control Peach leaf curl. Also provide cover from rain splash to prevent the spread of the disease.

-Continue to clear snow from fruit cages to prevent damage.

-Continue to check stored fruit and dispose of any that are showing signs of deterioration.

TREES & SHRUBS.

-Deciduous trees and shrubs can be pruned now when weather permits this to be done, they can also be planted out into their permanent position when weather permits.

-Heavy snow should be knocked of evergreens to prevent damage.

A GENERAL GUIDE TO FILLING YOUR GARDEN WITH

-Trees and shrubs can be planted out now. Prepare the ground well and dig deeply mixing in fertiliser and if the soil is in a poor condition add compost. If conditions are very wet and cold it will be better to wait until the weather improves. Try to complete all bare rooted trees, shrubs and roses by March, before the plants come back into growth

-Check newly planted trees and shrubs after hard frosts and heel in if necessary, to firm the ground around the root ball.

-Before growth begins, Pollarded trees can be pruned to keep them within manageable size.

-If rabbits are a problem, protect new trees with wire mesh or trunk bands to prevent lower bark being chewed off.

BULBS.

-Order your bulbs, corms and tubers to plant for summer flowers.

-Take care when hoeing and forking over borders not to damage developing bulbs.

-Keep a check on pot grown bulbs and do not allow them to become waterlogged or too dry. Protection will be needed during long spells of cold weather.

-Lilies can be potted up now to be planted out later when the weather improves.

-Snowdrops will still be in flower this month and can also be lifted and divided in spells of milder weather. Start to feed these now with a general fertiliser to build up a health bulb for next year.

-If you are looking for colour in your garden at this time of year there is a surprising amount to choose from and none easier to grow than from bulbs. Aconite, Cyclamen, Anemones, Crocus, Iris and Narcissus have all early varieties to choose from and are a welcome early splash of colour.

THE GREENHOUSE.

-Continue to bring in potted Strawberries to encourage early crops.

-Pelargoniums can be sown now in a heated propagator/windowsill.

-Overwintered Begonia tubers can be started back into growth in a heated propagator or on a windowsill.

-Remember to check greenhouse heaters every evening and refill.

-Spinach, Carrots, Radish, and spring onions can be sown in a greenhouse border.

-Broad beans, greenhouse Tomatoes, Onions, Celeriac, Brussels sprouts, Cabbages, Globe artichokes, and Lettuce can be sown in pots and trays.

THE POND.

-Ice can still be a problem this month. Use a pan of hot water placed on the ice to melt a breath hole for fish. Frogs can also overwinter in ponds and also will need to breath. Do not be tempted to break the ice because the shock wave could startle fish and kill them.

A GENERAL GUIDE TO FILLING YOUR GARDEN WITH

-Herons can be a welcome visitor to your garden, but they will be looking for lunch. Where you can prevent losses is by placing a terracotta ridge tile, or pipe into the pond to give your fish a hiding place.

-If snow falls during spells on your pond when being frozen, this can prevent light getting through. Clear off snow as soon as possible.

-Raised ponds will need the side protecting during heavy frost. Expanding ice can cause damage to the side and be difficult to repair, so prevention is better. Line the sides with old carpets and bubble wrap.

-If you are planning a pond soon and intend to have fish in it, aim for a depth of 3 ft minimum and at least 4 sq. metres. Temperatures will fluctuate in ponds any smaller and will most likely be unsuitable for fish.

-Bog gardens can be a useful extension to a pond and will increase the variety of plants available such as Caltha, Marsh Marigolds and Iris. They can also be a good solution to a particularly wet area in your garden if draining the area is not an option.

-Amphibians will be emerging from late march onwards and do their annual mating. If you are going to do any pond maintenance, then try to do this before March.

THE ROCK GARDEN.

-Just like last month, your Alpines will benefit from a top dressing of gravel or shingle to help

protect them from severe wet weather.
-Remember to correct waterlogged areas as mentioned in last month's section on Rock gardens.

LAWN CARE.

-Just like last month, in heavy spells of snow try to avoid piling this onto your lawn as this can damage the lawn underneath.
-If you are planning a new lawn in the spring, now is still a good time to prepare the ground and allow time for the soil to settle before laying/seeding the new lawn.
-Avoid walking on the lawn during spells of heavy frost.
-During heavy spells of rain you may find areas of your lawn that are waterlogged, make a note of these areas and correct later in the year by either air-rating by spiking the area, or if the area is seriously waterlogged, then a drainage system may need to be implemented.
-Check your lawn mower this month. Ensure blades are undamaged and sharp.
-It is still too soon to grow a lawn from seed, but weather permitting, lawns from turf can be laid.
-Dumps in lawns can be annoying and your lawn mower can leave them bare of grass. Use a sharp spade to cut an H pattern in the lawn. Peel back both sides and re-level the surface, then roll back the turf and firm back into place.

-Continue to mulch around plants to prevent

frosts damaging plants.

-Now is a good time to build a compost heap for the season ahead. Used pallets are a good and quick way to do this and can simply be strapped together to form you structure to form your compost bin.

-While plants are still dormant, now is a good time to apply wood preservative to your fences and do any general repairs that are needed.

-Try to complete all garden digging this month to give the frosts time to break down the soil and add plenty of organic matter.

-Now is also a good time to jet wash patios and paths to remove the build-up of algae to prevent them from becoming slippery and unsightly.

-February for wildlife can still be a harsh month. Many berry trees will now be bare and with prolonged cold spells, birds will struggle to obtain enough food. Do keep checking bird feeders daily and clear bird baths of ice. Spring can feel like it has also come early at times, but birds will still need feed to build up their reserves for the breeding season ahead.

-Many insects overwinter in our gardens and if you are doing a winter cleanup do spare a thought for these creatures. Many of them are beneficial to our gardens such as ground beetles that will seek out and eat many overwintering garden pests. If you do come across hibernating insects take care not to disturb them and you will be rewarded later in the year when they help to control pests, for free. Ladybirds can also be found grouped together in nooks and crannies so if you do come across these, again, do try to not disturb them.

-As previously mentioned in the January section on wildlife, many species are in decline, including native plants. This is happening on a worldwide scale and there is no doubt in my mind our gardens can help. When you look at how many gardens are available across the country, try to envisage how much land area is available for all of us to use in helping wildlife. If each gardener just did a few things to help wildlife, this will be magnified across the whole country and can only reward us all in the long term. Even in my lifetime I have seen a dramatic decline in wildlife species and would hate to think that future generations would never have the pleasure of seeing some of are spectacular wildlife. It may sound melodramatic, but don't take my word for it. Do your own research and you may be shocked into wanting to do more to help? Just by growing a few more plants that benefit insects and birds, creating places for wildlife to hibernate, growing flowers that provide the habitat that specific insects, butterflies, moths and many more need to reproduce will all help. Money in some respects doesn't come into this part of gardening, because many of the beneficial things we can be doing cost little to no money. Building insects homes from recycled materials lying around our gardens, sowing a wildflower border for the price of a packet of seed, just to name two. Your children will also enjoy the projects you can do for wildlife and by getting them involved you will also be educating them on the plight and the necessity to do more for our wildlife.

MARCH.

Spring can feel it has arrived, but at times will still feel a long way off. The days are stretching out faster now and by the end of the month a real change in our gardens can be seen. Spring bulbs can be seen everywhere we look, and Daffodils festoon our road verges. For me, March is an exciting month with plants starting to emerge from there winter slumber as the transition from Winter to Spring starts to happen. The better weather means other gardening jobs can be done at this time, like pruning roses and providing we don't have too much rain, the first lawn mowing can be done. As in February, it can be tempting to try to get too far ahead and start planting out tender plants because milder weather can feel like Winter has finally behind us. This again can be a mistake and plants will still need protecting from a sudden cold snap that will undo all your hard work. It can be difficult to gauge what the weather will be like from week to week so do take precautions against sudden cold snaps, especially with young seedlings which can be wiped out in a single frosty night if left unprotected.

A GENERAL GUIDE TO FILLING YOUR GARDEN WITH FLOWERS.

-March is the optimum time to prune Roses. Where you live, will depend on when to prune. Further north, prune later, further south prune earlier. The reason for this is that, prune to early and a late frost will damage young shoots, prune too late and growth that has been put on will have to be pruned out, spending the plant's energy. Modest pruning can be done during Winter to shorten stems to reduce rose rock. If cold weather persists, delaying pruning for a week or two will do no harm to the plant. Begin pruning by taking out all dead material and any diseased stems. Remove crossing stems on Hybrid Teas and Floribundas, then shorten the main stems to promote strong new shoots to grow from the base of the bush.

-Continue to sow summer annuals such as Ageratum, Antirrhinum, Begonia, Impatiens Marigolds, Nasturtium, Pelargonium, Petunias, sweat Peas and Zinnia can be sown in a heated propagator or a sunny windowsill.

-Hardy annuals to sow outside in well-prepared sites in full sun are Calendula, Godetia, Larkspur, and Nigella.

-Half hardy annual to sow this month, Ageratum, Alyssum, Begonia, Sempervirens, Brachycome, Cleome, Gerbera, Heliotrope, Impatiens, Kochia, Marigold, Nemesia, Nicotinia, Pelargonium, Petunia, Tagetes and Verbena. Delay planting in colder areas until later this month unless heat can be provided.

-Continue to water Pelargoniums and re-pot overwintered plants.

-Continue to water Fuchsias, trim back to 3 inches and re-pot overwintered plants.

-Keep an eye on new seedlings to avoid overcrowding and prick out as soon as two leaves have formed.

-Dahlias can be started into to growth now and use new shoots for cuttings if you want to increase stocks. Trim 2-3-inch shoots, trim off bottom leaves and make a clean cut just below a joint. Pot in gritty compost and water in. Place in propagator to root. Pot up tubers and gradually increase watering.

-Heathers that have finished flowering can be given a trim to promote bushy growth.

-Now is a good time to trim back all dead top growth on perennials that flowered last season.

-Hardy Fuchsias can be pruned back now in milder areas.

-Hydrangeas can also be pruned back, but again in colder climates leave last year's top growth to protect young emerging shoots.

-Winter Jasmine can be pruned once it had finished flowering.

-Continue to dead head winter flowering Pansies, Violas, and Primulas.

-Now is a good time to divide overgrown border plants. Spilt into smaller sections and discard tired and worn out centres. Replant into well-rotted manured or compost enriched sites.

-Now is a good time to apply a general fertiliser to borders and add a layer of manure, forked into the surface.

VEGETABLES.

-Beetroot, Broad beans, Brussels Sprouts, early Carrots, Lettuce, Radish, Spring Onions, Spinach, Turnips, Parsnips and early Peas can be sown under cloches.

-Cauliflowers, Celery, Leeks, Onions, summer Cabbage and early Tomatoes can be sown in the greenhouse.

-Leeks can be sown now under glass for planting out in April.

-Parsnips can also still be planted now until April.

-Plant Onion sets 4 inches apart in 9 to 12-inch rows.

-Early Potatoes can be planted now. Plant 5 inches deep, 10 to 12 inches apart in rows 24 inches apart.

-Sow Broad beans 3 inches deep, 4 inches apart in rows 10 inches apart.

-Begin to harden off greenhouse grown Onions, Lettuce, Summer cabbage and Brussels sprouts.

-Remove old crops and add to compost heap.

-Continue to dig over vacant ground from cleared crops adding in well-rotted manure or compost as you dig.

-Set out early varieties of Potatoes in seed trays.

Place in a light, cool place to develop shoots.
-Prepare your Runner Bean beds now, adding plenty of manure and compost.
-Cover Rhubarb crowns with large terracotta pots to encourage early stems for pulling.

FRUIT.

-Bare rooted, canes or pot grown fruit trees and bushes can still be planted out now. Delay planting if the ground is frozen or wet.
-Aim to finish all fruit tree pruning this month.
-Raspberries that fruited in the Autumn should be cut back to ground level by now.
-Continue to cover outdoor Strawberries to encourage an early crop.

-Spray peaches with a fungicide to prevent Peach leaf curl. Pot grown specimens can be brought into the greenhouse for early flowering.
-Protect early blossoms from frosts with horticultural fleece or a fine netting.
-Now is the time to cover fruiting plants with fruit cages and netting to protect from birds damaging buds. Finches particularly like stripping buds from Gooseberries, these can also be pruned now. Aim to create an open branched structure to let in light an air.
-Feed all fruit trees with sulphate of potash fertiliser.

TREES & SHRUBS.

-Inspect your tree stakes, and firm in if loose, replace if they have rotted and check ties to see if they are too tight.

-Ensure you have completed pruning deciduous trees now that growth has started again.

-Dogwoods and decorative colour bark willows can be pruned to within 6 inches of their base.

-Pot grown specimens roots may have become congested, tease out the roots before planting to encourage the roots to spread out from the root ball.

-Continue to mulch round trees and shrubs.

-Control early attacks of aphids with an insecticide.

THE GREENHOUSE.

-Indoor Tomatoes, Cucumbers, Melons, Aubergines and Peppers can be sown if you can provide warmth in the greenhouse or sunny windowsill.

-Don't leave bags of compost outside, bring into the greenhouse and allow it to warm up before using.

-Wash old plant labels and re-use.

-When sowing small seeds, you can use fine vermiculite to cover them to make it easier for germinating plants to reach the surface.

-Invest in a small thermometer to check your propagator is operating at the right temperature.

-Ventilate the greenhouse whenever the weather permits to avoid damp air build up and spreading disease.

-If you have not already done so, clean greenhouse glass and wash down staging. Clean used pots and do any repairs to glass panes. Line your greenhouse with bubble wrap to preserve heat.

-Snow drops can be lifted and divided when they have finished flowering.
-Lilies can be planted into pots now or in borders. They like free draining soil of plant onto a layer of grit.

LAWN CARE.

-Keep off lawns when it is frosty also when it is wet to avoid damaging it.
-In milder areas your lawn may be starting to grow. Check the mower blades are set high before mowing.
-Moss in your lawn can be tackled now. Rake it out gently and an herbicide can be applied. Once the remaining moss has blackened, rake this out as well.

-Continue to mulch around plants to prevent frosts damaging plants.
-Now is still a good time to build a compost heap for the season ahead.
-While plants are still dormant, now is still a good time to apply wood preservative to your fences and do any general repairs that are needed.
-Try to complete all garden digging this month adding plenty of organic matter.

A GENERAL GUIDE TO FILLING YOUR GARDEN WITH

- Weeds will begin in earnest to wage war on the garden. On dry days using a sharp-edged hoe, sever them at ground level. Aim to do this regularly from now on to stop them growing too large and leeching nutrients from your soil. Mulch liberally to suppress them.

- Now is still a good time to jet wash patios and paths to remove the build-up of algae to prevent them from becoming slippery and unsightly.

- Wash all canes and stakes that have been used last year to prevent the spread of disease.

- Clean all pruning equipment after each pruning session and keep blades sharp. Blunt tools damage stems and will encourage disease to enter a poorly pruned stem and also increase the chances of die back.

- One worrying trend I want to high-light this month is land development. With an ever-increasing population more and more houses are being built. This of course is necessary, but does little for wildlife and worst of all is the volume of houses that are being crammed into the spaces they are being built, hence the gardens are becoming so small that in some cases the gardens resemble the size of a small patio. These gardens will obviously struggle to create the biodiversity that a normal sized garden has and secondly leaves the owner with little to no gardening to do and negates the necessity to garden and learn about gardening. This doesn't mean to say these smaller spaces cannot be valuable, but it does detract from good practice on developing our land more responsibly to preserve wildlife. Having said that, it is even more important to learn about how we can provide habitats for wildlife within these smaller spaces. This does not mean you need to let your garden go wild and become a miniature jungle to help and encourage wild, it merely means you will need to utilise this space more wisely to benefit you, and your local wildlife. One of the plights of our most iconic mammals is the hedgehog. These have been in decline for many years, but with some careful consideration can still be a regular visitor to your garden. If you have just bought your house and have a shoe box size garden with garish six-foot panels on all sides, the first thing to consider is access. This is simple to do. Remove a panel or two and cut a small access hole. Replace the panel, job done. It is also a good idea to encourage all you neighbours to do the same and highlight what and why you are doing it. If the sight of the hole bothers you, just plant a shrub next to it and it will be like it was never there. Utilise your fences by growing climbers and in particular Ivy. There are many decorative leaved varieties to choose from and where Ivy comes into its own is the volume of insects it supports. Many uses it to hibernate and once established birds also like it to nest in. A bird table and birth bath will also help during the Winter months and placed adjacent to your kitchen window or patio, will not only give you hours of pleasure watching them from the comfort of your own home, you will be also helping to support many struggling species that are sadly also in decline. Pot plants also become a good staple in a small garden, not only can fruit trees be grown in them, you can also create mini rock garden displays in troughs and because you can choose the compost they grow in, it opens up many possibilities of a wider range of plants. Just because you have a small garden, don't think growing your own vegetables is out the question. Not all Tomatoes, Cucumbers, Chilli Peppers and many more, need a greenhouse and many plants now are available to grow outdoors will yield excellent crops and have been specifically bred to be grown outside. By choosing varieties of plants that attract Butterflies will also help, and a Buddleia will be a magnet for Butterflies when in flower and let's not forget herbs. Not only are they great insect attractors, like lavender and tansy, we can use them as well. Creating an insect home, adding a water feature, or just filling a pot with a wildflower seed mix will all help. If the trend of gardens becoming smaller and smaller continues, then it will become even more important we all try to do something to assist in the survival of our wildlife. We ignore this at our peril. When I see documentaries of farmers having to hire beehives to pollinate crops, surely this rings alarm bells that we need to act now and not wait until it is too late.

APRIL.

With the days lengthening, trees and bulbs in full bloom everywhere spring feels like it has finally arrived. The weather can still yield some nasty frosts and even snow, so again, be cautious with tender plants and if you are planting them out, they will still need protection. Towards the end of this month it will be time to start thinking about hardening off those plants raised in your greenhouse. Make room in your cold frame or ensure you have a warm sunny area, sheltered from the wind in your garden to place them. Also, have a fleece ready each night in case a frost is forecast. Better still, ensure you have adequate space remaining in the greenhouse to put them back inside during bad weather.

FLOWERS.

-Finish the sowing of hardy annuals to sow outside this month in well-prepared sites in full sun such as Calendula, Godetia, Larkspur, and Nigella.
-Finish sowing half-hardy annuals this month such as Ageratum, Alyssum, Begonia, Sempervirens, Brachycome, Cleome, Gerbera, Heliotrope,

A GENERAL GUIDE TO FILLING YOUR GARDEN WITH

Impatiens, Kochia, Marigold, Nemesia, Nicotinia, Pelargonium, Petunia, Tagetes and Verbena. Delay planting in colder areas until later this month unless heat can be provided.

-Remove dead heads off Hydrangeas, remove weak stems. Trim back slightly to a pair of new shoots, Hydrangea Paniculata can be trimmed to about half of last season's growth to a pair of new shoots.

-Buddleia if left can grow large. To contain their size prune to 12 inches from ground level.

-Sweet Peas can be planted directly outside now. Provide them with support.

-Clear top growth of Perennials. New growth should now be coming from the base.

-Roses struck in Autumn may need firming in, remove suckers before they grow to large. Feed all species now with a high potash fertiliser. Spray now to combat black spot with a fungicide.

-Trim Lavenders, Olearia, Euonymus and Viburnum to promote bushy growth removing any leggy or dead material.

-Now is a good time to transplant Azaleas and Rhododendrons. Prepare new sites well, fertilise with blood fish and bone meal adding plenty of organic matter to the new hole. Firm in and water well, mulch to conserve moisture and prevent weeds growing.

-Begin hardening off summer Annuals and Perennials. Move them to a cold frame or shelter area, cover with fleece if frosts are expected.

-Keep checking Heathers and as soon as flowers

finish, trim back by around a third.

-Begin hardening of early flowering Chrysanthemums in well-prepared soil. Delay if frosts persist.

-If you have a border that is dry and sunny, choose plants that thrive in these locations such as Arctotis, Mesembryantheumum, Phacelia and Portulaca Grandiflora.

-Slugs and snails will be out and about now so check regularly for damage on newly planted young plants before they undo all your hard work.

VEGETABLES.

-Plants to sow directly outside under cover are, Beetroot, Broad beans, Brussels Sprouts, Leeks, early Carrots, Main crop Carrots, Lettuce, Radish, Spring Onions, Spinach, Turnips, Parsnips and early Peas.

-Plants to sow in a heated propagator or sunny windowsill are, Aubergines, Tomatoes, Celery and Cauliflowers and Peppers.

-Potatoes to plant now are early varieties 12 inches apart and main crop potatoes 15 inches apart, remember to earth up to protect new shoots from late frosts.

-Onions and Shallots can be planted outside now, plant to soil level, and firm in. Netting or fleece may be needed to prevent birds pulling them out of the ground. Remove once strong growth begins.

-To prevent attacks of Carrot root fly, protect plants with fleece and bury the edging. Also, you can construct a 2 feet high screen around plants.

A GENERAL GUIDE TO FILLING YOUR GARDEN WITH

Marigolds are also a good companion plant.

-Now is a good time to begin sowing herbs such as Chives, Fennel, Marjoram and thyme. Lavender hedges are a good garden hedge for protecting low growing plants from wind damage. They prefer poorer soils so resist improving the soil. Trim plants hard back after the first year to promote bushy growth.

-Continue to cover Strawberries with cloches for early crops.
-Protect Gooseberries from birds with netting.
-Begin fulling stems from Rhubarb you forced earlier in the year.
-Protect fruit blossoms with netting or fleece if frosts are forecast.

-Now is a good time to plant Evergreens including ground-covering and slow growing Conifers, Hollies and Laurels, as they have started back into growth. If you are planning a new hedge, prepare the soil well and water in dry spells.
-Check newly plants trees and shrubs that the ties are secure and not to tight, firm back in if the weather has caused wind rock.

BULBS.

-Begin starting to plant Gladiola corms this month until May. Stagger planting for successive blooms.
-Lily-of-the-valley crowns can be dug up and divided this month. Prepare the soil well before re-

planting. Crown can be bought at good garden centres.

-Top-dress emerging bulbs with an all-round fertiliser to promote good blooms.

-Regularly hand weed around bulbs to prevent damage by hoeing.

-Container grown bulbs must not be allowed to dry out or flowers may fail to bloom

-Plant summer flowering bulbs such as Cannas, Dutch Iris and Lilies.

THE GREENHOUSE.

-Begin pricking out plants sown earlier.

-Cuttings taken last year can now be potted on.

-Take cutting from new shoots of Pelargoniums and Fuchsias.

-Pinch put Fuchsia tips to encourage bushy growth, increase watering and feed every two weeks.

-Re-pot overwintered plants to encourage new growth.

-Basil can be sow now but will need protecting from frosts.

-Globe Artichokes do better when established in spring. Space them 3 feet apart in rows of 3 feet and set the crowns at soil level.

-Keep the greenhouse and cold frame glass clean to maximise light.

-Whitefly, Aphids and Red spider mite need immediate treatment if discovered to prevent serious outbreaks.

A GENERAL GUIDE TO FILLING YOUR GARDEN WITH

-Ventilate the greenhouse freely from now on but remember to close windows at night.

THE POND.

-Amphibians will be emerging from late March onwards to do their annual mating. If you are going to do any pond maintenance, then try to do this before March.

-Pond lilies in baskets can be planted during mild weather. Take into account which variety you have bought because planting depths need to be correct. Miniature varieties plant at 9 inches, small varieties plant to 12 inches, medium varieties at 18 inches and some larger varieties can be planted at 36 inches.

-Remove blanket weed before it becomes established, use a forked branch.

-Alpines lifted by frosts or lacking vigour will need replanting. Ensure soil is free draining and if waterlogged, add plenty of grit.

LAWN CARE.

-Boost your lawn by aerating the surface by forking. Apply a spring fertiliser feed and weed. If using a selective weed killer, then water your lawn if it has not rained for more than two days.

-If you have not already done so, rake over your lawn to remove moss. Remember, broad leaf weed killers also kill all broad-leaved plants, so be careful when applying.

- If your lawn is bare and thin, re-seed over the lawn.
- Weather permitting, mow your lawn. Aim to set your mower blades no lower than 1 inch.
- Weather permitting, aim to mow your lawn at least once a week by the end of this month. Regular mowing will always be the best way for a lush lawn, and it will be more resistant to wear-and-tear and your lawn will be better able to cope with dry spells.

- Continue to mulch around plants to prevent frosts damaging plants.
- Keep checking plant supports and replace if necessary, also continue to tie in new shoots.
- Now is still a good time to build a compost heap for the season ahead. Used pallets are a good and quick way to do this and can simply be strapped together to form you structure to form your compost bin.
- Some plants may still be dormant, apply wood preservative to your fences avoiding splashing plants coming into growth, and do any general repairs that are needed.
- Weed borders on dry days using a sharp-edged hoe, sever them at ground level. Aim to do this regularly from now on to stop them growing too large and leeching nutrients from your soil. Mulch liberally to suppress them.
- Now is still a good time to jet wash patios and paths to remove the build-up of algae to prevent

them from becoming slippery and unsightly.
-Continue washing all canes and stakes before using them to prevent the spread of disease.
-Clean all pruning equipment after each pruning session and keep blades sharp. Blunt tools damage stems and will encourage disease to enter a poorly pruned stem and also increase the chances of die back.

-Spring will be in full flow this month and along with the surge in plant growth many species of life will be coming out of their winter hiding places with the longer days and warmer temperatures.
-Continue feeding birds to boost their energy levels as the nest building and breeding season gets underway.
-Unless you are after a show lawn, try to avoid spraying weed killers in spring. Many species use this to construct their nests and the chemicals could harm the young.
-Mammals will be more active this month and if you are lucky enough to have hedgehogs and want to encourage them to nest in your garden, then place a saucer of cat food out for them. Do remember if you are encouraging hedgehogs into your garden you cannot use slug pellets.
-Make the effort to go out into your garden in early morning or evening to have a better chance of spotting, Foxes, Badgers, Hedgehogs and Bats.
-Many insects will be emerging this month and overwintering, Peacock, Tortoiseshell, Brim-

stone and Red admirals will be looking for an energy replacing fix of nectar. Encourage them into your garden by planting early flowering plants such as Grape hyacinth, Pulmonaria.

-Ladybirds will also be emerging on warmer days and will be looking for aphids to feed on. Nettles may not be every gardener favourite weed, but many insects and butterflies use them for feasting on aphids and laying eggs on for their larva to feed on, if, where you can, leave a small patch to grow and later in the year you can harvest the nettles, place in a water butt for a few days and use this as a free plant tonic.

-Woodlands are magical places in Spring and this month sees in the beginning of the show with Bluebells, Anemones and clumps of Lesser Celandine putting on their springtime flower displays.

MAY.

Spring is well underway now and the garden will be going through a huge transformation with the bulk of growth being put on during the next few months. With plants going into overdrive, weeds included, the best policy to adopt at this time of year is little and often. A good tip is to walk around your garden and take notes on all those jobs you have piling up. Then once you have an idea of everything you want to achieve, try to set aside time for each task. It is surprising how the smallest of job can take up a lot of your spare time. By allocating specific days and times for these jobs around the garden you will be better placed at keeping on top of everything and be more organised. This will apply more so to those of you with a large garden, which can easily get away from you and become to larger a task to tackle. Be flexible with this approach because like all gardeners the weather is our task master and will dictate what, and when we can do on any given day. Again, little and often, is key to success in any garden and never more so at this time of year.

FLOWERS

- Continue to sow Hardy Annuals in well-prepared soil.
- Prick out any remaining seedlings to grow on in the greenhouse or cold frame.
- Now is hanging basket season and it's to start getting them ready to put out over the next few weeks. Do a check list to make you have everything you need before starting to plant up your baskets. Remember, many hanging basket plants are tender, so keep them in the greenhouse until all risk of frost is over.
- Bedding plants grown in the greenhouse can start being hardened of this month. Delay this if frosts are still persistent.
- Daily check for plants drying out as the temperatures can rise significantly in the greenhouse on sunny days.
- Continue dead heading Spring bedding.
- You can now start sowing sweat Peas directly into borders.
- If you have not started Dahlia tubers into growth in pots then plant the tubers directly outside.
- Perennials such as Ajuga, Alchemilla Euphorbia and Stachys that spread, cuttings can be taken now. Check the new shoots have roots, then simply pot up and water in well.
- Tall Herbaceous Perennials will begin to need supporting as growth is put on.
- Hoe regularly to remove Annual weeds and dig

out Perennial weeds such as Dock and Bramble.

-Prepare borders you want to plant Summer bedding. Remove any Spring bedding that has gone past its best.

-Bedding plants ordered by post should be opened straight away. Check for watering and keep in a warm, light place ready to be potted on ready to be potted out in early June.

VEGETABLES

-Continue to make regular sowing of Lettuce, Radish, Spring Onions and salad crops for a continuous supply, thus avoiding a glut.

-Sow main crop carrots outside and provide protection to keep off carrot root fly.

-Earth up shoots of Potatoes to protect from frosts and to increase yields.

-Sweetcorn can be sow in pots in a heated greenhouse or sunny windowsill.

-Aim to complete the sowing of Onion sets this month.

FRUIT

-Early blooms will still need protecting from frosts.

-Protect Strawberries as they begin to flower with a mulch of straw. Hoe the ground thoroughly and apply a thick mulch to prevent mud splash, if late frosts are forecast then cover plants with the straw.

-Spring flowering plants will benefit from pruning

after flowering. They will put on new growth this season for next year's blooms. Prune out very old woody branches and trim flowering shoots that have finished flowering.

-Check all trees for suckers and prune these out as close to the base as possible.

-Check fruit cages for holes.

-Continue spraying Peaches to protect against Peach leaf curl.

-Check over all your variegated plants and prune any that are reverting to green foliage.

-Continue to plant out container grown plants in well-prepared soil, water thoroughly and mulch.

-Feed your Spring flowering bulbs with a general fertiliser or liquid feed, continue dead heading flowers. Water during dry spells.

-Continue planting Gladioli corms to ensure successive flowering, aim to complete this by the end of this month.

THE GREENHOUSE

-Marrows and Courgettes can be sown. Sow in pairs and germinate in a warm place.

-Tomatoes Peppers and Cucumbers can be potted into their final growing places.

-Begin pricking out any remaining seedling.

-Plant out Early Summer Cauliflowers after hardening off.

-Begin sowing seed for Hardy Bi-annuals such as Forget-me-nots, Foxgloves.

-The greenhouse will need shading on hot days to prevent plants getting scorched.

THE POND

Introducing water into your garden can be very rewarding visually and will benefit your local wildlife tremendously. Here are some helpful tips to put you on the right path.

-Aim to have your pond in full sun and away from deciduous tree and if you know where the prevailing wind is coming from, aim to provide a barrier or hedge.

-Aim for minimum depth of 18 inches. Shallow pond is prone to temperature fluctuations and encourage blanket weed. If you want to have fish, then a depth of 36 inches is preferable and aim to have this as most of the depth and not just a small area in the centre.

-If using concrete instead of a liner then use a sealant to prevent lime leeching into the water.

-Before introducing fish allow plants to naturalise also allowing nitrates to disperse from filling your new pond with tap water. This can take over four weeks so be patient before adding fish.

-Oxygenating plants are essential along with floating plants. Use a variety in case you have failures. They will need pruning back in Autumn if they become to invasive.

-If you are planting water lilies, plant them at depths gradually to allow the plant to acclimatise to their final depth, allowing time for the leaves to reach the water surface.

-If you decide to have fish remember the waterfall or fountain will need to be kept running during hot spells especially overnight to keep the water oxygenated.

-A healthy sediment will develop over time, but you don't want too many Autumn drop leaves entering your pond which can pollute your pond when the leaves begin to rot. Prevent this by netting your pond during the leaf fall season.

-Now is a good time to divide and replant pond plants that are overgrown and replant them in baskets. Be careful if you have Amphibians, such as frogs and toads, not to disturb their spawn.

-Check your water pump is working correctly and clean out filters. Make sure all electrical cable is in good condition and replace any showing signs of deterioration.

-Remove blanket weed as soon as it has been spotted. With the warmer weather it can grow rapidly and take over ponds.

LAWN CARE

-This month is the optimum time to sow or lay a new lawn. With the warmer weather conditions the lawn will establish quicker. For seed and turf the preparation is the same. Prepare the site at least a month in advance. Dig over thoroughly, removing any Perennial weed roots. Firm down by treading steadily across the area, try not to overdo this and compact the soil. Level to an inch about where you want your new lawn level. This will allow for settling later on. Rake over removing any rocks or large stones. One week before sowing or laying your lawn apply a pre-sowing or laying fertiliser. If you intend to use seed, choose the right blend for your usage. A show lawn is better sown with a blend of seed containing various Fescues and Bent grasses and will not stand up to heavy wear. For a domestic or everyday day lawn choose a blend containing Rye varieties of grass that will withstand hardware. Follow the manufacturers sowing ratios carefully to avoid patchy areas. Protection will be needed form birds. A simple way is to use netting pegged down with plant pots underneath to raise it off the ground, specialist lawn fleece can also be bought that allows the grass to grow through and stops broad leaved weed growth. Lawn turf comes in grades from specialist growers. Do be careful when buying cheap or inferior lawn turf because this can be meadow turf that has been simply cut off a field and passed off as good quality turf and may-well contain many unwanted weeds and pests. Ensure you are ready to lay the new lawn as soon as it arrives. If you are delayed, then do be aware that after seven days the rolled-up lawn will deteriorate quickly, yellow and even die. Stagger laying into a brick like formation and aim to lay as larger pieces at the edges, because short end cuts will dry out quickly and shrivel. Lay the turf by standing on a plant of wood to avoid damaging it. Tamp down the lawn after laying or walk along the plank of wood, flip over and repeat. Water in well and continue watering every seven to ten days if it has not rained.

-A general good rule to follow for a good, thick, quality lawn is to mow regularly. Change the direction with each cut to ensure even cutting of the grass, for fine lawns a second pass at right angles will ensure a more even finish.

-If like many of us you enjoy attracting wildlife into your garden there is no better way than leaving your grass to grow. You can mow around the edges and a pathway through it to keep it looking like you have done this intentionally and your neighbours don't think you have left your garden to go wild. If this doesn't appeal to you, then just leave a few square metres in a quiet corner. Longer grass will attract many butterflies such as the Meadow Brown, Gatekeeper, Small Heath and the Common Blue and you may even attract Damsel flies. Grassland flowers are also a great way to introduce more wildlife into your garden. By allowing wildflowers like Ribwort Plantain, Red clover, Meadow Cranesbill, and Ox-eye daisies that can either be planted into or allowed to naturalist in your lawn, will all attract more insects into your garden. For established lawns a better way to plant wildflowers is to grow a wild seed mix in pots and spot plant out later when they have grown larger and can compete better with the grasses.

JUNE.

The garden can feel like it is changing on a daily basis now that Summer is finally here and with the plants you have raised putting on so much growth it is important to keep on top of all the good work you have been doing in the garden. Watering will become a main priority as the days heat up along with weeding and keeping the lawn regularly mown. Pests will be also having a feast on your plants so do keep an eye out for those and take precautions sooner rather than later to avoid infestations. There is still plenty to do and plenty of seed sowing still to be done so don't ease off on the gas and keep up all the good work to ensure your garden is looking tip-top and teaming with plants that look healthy and ready to give you the fruits of all you hard efforts.

FLOWERS.

-Continue planting Summer Half-Hardy Annuals and Perennials in well-prepared soil. Ensure they are fully hardened off before planting out.

-Continue sowing your Bi-annuals until the end of July, plants such as Foxgloves, Sweet Williams,

Forget-me-nots and Canterbury bells.

-Congested clumps of Polyanthus and Primulas can now be dug up and divided.

-Begin routinely dead heading spent flowers to prolong their season.

-Roses will need routinely checking for disease and pests such as aphids. Spray every few weeks if needed with a fungicide and insecticide combination. Clear all dead leaves away from the base and cut away any suckers as soon as spotted. New shoots growing on climbers and rambling Roses need to be tied in. Hoe Rose fertiliser into the ground around each bush. Mulch.

-Hydrangea cuttings can be taken now. Take cutting with no flowering buds showing and root on in a heated propagator.

-Continue planting up hanging baskets and grow on in the greenhouse keeping them well watered.

-Sow Winter flowering Pansies now for planting out in the Autumn.

-Acid loving plants will benefit from an acid fertiliser. This can be spread or watered in plants such as Rhododendrons, Camellias, Azaleas and Pieris to ensure strong growth and prevent leaves yellowing.

-Continue pinching out tips on Chrysanthemums to promote branching and more flowering stems.

VEGETABLES.

-Plants to sow outside from May to early June are Broad Beans, French Beans, Runner Beans Cab-

A GENERAL GUIDE TO FILLING YOUR GARDEN WITH

bages, Beetroot, Calabrese, Carrots, Cauliflowers, Kale, Lettuce, Radish, Kohl Rabi, Peas, Mange Tout, Spinach, Sweetcorn, Swiss Chard Turnips and Fennel.

-Keep drawing up soil on Potatoes to encourage roots to grow from the stem to increase crops.

-Thin out seedlings planted in rows outside to correct their spacing.

-Outdoor varieties of cucumber can be planted outside now, provide protection with a cloche.

-Runner beans that have been raised under glass can be planted outside now. Seed can be directly sown outside. Sow two seeds 2 inches deep, 9 inches apart, remove the weaker seedling after germination allowing one plant per cane spacing.

-Self blanching Celery should be planted in blocks and standard varieties, in deep trenches to be earth up later on.

-Tomatoes sown in Feb/Mar can be planted out now. Ensure there are no late frosts as they are not frost hardy and will need protecting. If soil conditions are still cold, delay planting. If planting in the greenhouse then ensure pot grow plants have a pot size no less than 12 inches.

-Sweetcorn raised in pots earlier can be planted outside. Plant in blocks rather than rows 12 inches apart for better pollination and more successful crops.

-Brussels Sprouts can now be planted into their final beds along with Summer and Autumn Varieties of Cabbage.

-Complete Potato planting this month, and earth up new shoots to encourage higher yields.

-Leeks can be planted outside. Plant them 6 inches apart in rows 12 inches apart. Plant them 5 to 6 inches deep using a dibber and water in. Shorten leaves by half.

FRUIT.

-Gooseberries, pick some smaller fruits now will encourage the remaining fruits to grow larger.

-Raspberry plants, tie in new shoots and remove any that are creeping across your beds.

-Blackberry shoots will be growing from the base, so ties these in for your fruits next year.

-Strawberries grown under cover need pollinating when in flower so remove cloches to allow access for insects to pollinate. Tidy up early fruiting varieties after fruiting has stopped.

-Apples that suffer from scab or powdery mildew will need spraying every two weeks.

-Net bushes to prevent birds eating fruits.

-If the weather is dry, water plants, especially newly established trees and bushes.

-Check on fruit laden trees, thin if required.

-Tie in new shoots of fan trained trees.

-Summer prune bush and cordon trained Gooseberries, Red and White currants by shortening the side shoots back to five leaves.

-Keep an eye out for Mildew and spray with an appropriate fungicide.

-Water fruiting bushes well in dry spells to keep

fruits swelling. Try to keep water off the leaves to reduce fungal diseases.

TREES & SHRUBS.

-Now is a time to give Privet hedges their first cut. A tip to make the job easier is to lay a sheet or tarpaulin to collect the clipping as you go.

-Many Spring and Summer flowering shrubs can be pruned after flowering such as Philadelphus and Ribes. To promote thick growth and avoiding woody stems aim to prune back by a third. With doing this each year it will prevent the leaves becoming smaller and promote better flowering

-Keep an eye on newly planted trees and shrubs for drying out and water regularly.

-Tidy Hedges such as Privet, yews and Lonicera by pruning long new shoots.

-Once Broom has finished flowering, shorten new growth being careful not to cut back into old wood.

-If you require the space for bedding in your borders you can lift Spring flowering bulbs. They will still need time to fatten up the bulbs for next year. Make a temporary home by digging a trench, then covering the bulbs where they can be left to grow on.

-Begin lifting and drying Tulips and Hyacinth bulbs.

THE GREENHOUSE.

-Now is a good time to take cutting such as Pelargoniums and Fuchsias.

-Tomatoes will need watering regularly and side shoots nipping off cordon varieties. Tap flowering plants to encourage pollination and once the first fruits have set, start feeding weekly.

-Marrows and Courgettes can be planted from late May to early June.

-Watch out for Vine Weevil, adult beetles maybe active around potted plants.

-As soon as the Summer heat begins, shading may be needed. Use a painted wash or netting.

-Ensure watered plants are not sitting in cold water overnight and encouraging disease. Try to water early in the morning to avoid this problem.

-Misting Peppers will help to set fruit.

THE POND.

-Overgrown plants may become a problem as the season gets underway so if you like a neat and tidy pond then being ruthless is the only solution. Blanket and Duckweed can also be a problem. These are best removed manually by using a small branch or a cane with nails in the end for the Blanket weed and a sturdy net for the Duckweed.

-If Algae blooms keep occurring due to the increase in temperature, then ensure you have enough oxygenating plants such as Potamogeton Crispusm or Elodea Canadensis to starve out the algae of nutrients and promoting clear water.

A GENERAL GUIDE TO FILLING YOUR GARDEN WITH

LAWN CARE.

-Apply a lawn fertiliser to give your lawns a boast.
-If required apply a weed and moss killer. Avoid adding these clippings to your compost heap.
-If you are planning lawn later in the year, now is a good time to start preparing the soil.
-In really dry spells, higher the blades on your mower and leave the clippings on the lawn to conserve moisture.
-Aerate compacted areas by applying sharp sand and loam then feeding with a high Nitrogen fertiliser.
-Weeds killer should be avoided using in very dry spells. Wait until Autumn.
-Continue to cut the lawn at least once a week for hard wearing lawns and show lawns at least twice a week.

JULY.

With the height of Summer arriving so is the need to keep watering all those precious plants you have so diligently looked after all year. Some days can get really hot now and no more so in the greenhouse and cold frame. Watering regularly will have to be on a daily basis in order for you to get the most out of your plants. Fruits and vegetables will need to be kept on eye on for pests and disease and keep dead heading those flowers for prolonged Summer flowering. There is still plenty to do but, remember why you are doing it. Take time out to relax and enjoy your garden with a glass or two of your favourite drink and savour the Summers long days and warm evenings.

FLOWERS.

-Finish planting Summer Half-Hardy Annuals and Perennials in well-prepared soil. Ensure they are fully hardened off before planting out.
-Continue sowing your Bi-annuals until the end of this month, plants such as Foxgloves, Sweet Williams, Forget-me-nots and Canterbury bells.
-Continue to take cutting of plants such as

A GENERAL GUIDE TO FILLING YOUR GARDEN WITH Fuchsias, Pelargonium, Hydrangea and Osteospermum.

- Continue spraying Roses with a fungicide and insecticide mix to prevent problems.
- Thin out Hardy Annuals you have sown directly into a border and transplant to fill in gaps.
- Dead head border plants such as Lupins, Delphiniums and Campanula as soon as flowering has finished. Trim flowering spikes right back to the base.
- Continue sowing seed for Winter colour such as Winter Pansies, Browalia, Calceolaria, Cineraria, and Schizanthus.
- Finish planting out tender plants this month. They should not need protecting and any cloches can be removed.
- Fill empty gaps in your borders.
- Hanging baskets should be also be finished planted this month, as soon as flowers die, dead head to prolong flowering
- Pot on cuttings when their roots have filled the pot.
- Keep spraying against mildew and use a powerful jet of water from a hose pipe to knock of infestations of pests like Aphids.
- Continue to stake and tie in tall plants such as Sun flowers.
- Regularly pick Sweet Pea seed heads to promote flowering.
- Do not let Begonias dry out, or they drop their flowers.

-Feed plants weekly with a high potash fertiliser.

VEGETABLES.

-Crops to sow this month are Peas, Lettuce, Radish, Beetroot, Runner Beans, Kohlrabi, Spinach, French Beans Chinese Cabbage, Spring Onions and Carrots.

-Marrows and Courgettes can be planted outside and keep them well watered.

-Finish pulling Rhubarb by mid-July then leave to allow the plant time to build up strength for next season.

-Early Potatoes will be ready to harvest soon, check a single plant and if too small leave to continue to grow and water regularly in dry spells.

-Onions should never be left to dry out or the yield will be severely reduced, water regularly in dry spells and keep weeds at bay regular hoeing between plants being careful not to damage the bulbs.

-Finish planting out Sweetcorn this month, remembering to plant in blocks to promote better pollination.

-Cut off flowering spikes of Rhubarb when they begin to form.

-Cauliflower leaves can be bent over to protect curds from sun scorch.

-Start sowing Winter Spinach.

-Brussels Sprouts can be planted into their final growing positions and plant them at least 30 inches apart.

A GENERAL GUIDE TO FILLING YOUR GARDEN WITH

-Start sowing String Cabbage in pots or nursery beds to plant out later.

-Continue thinning to correct spacings. Use the spare plants for any gaps in the rows.

FRUIT.

-This month birds will be trying to feast on your ripening fruits, so net wherever possible.

-Keep a close eye on your borders, weeds can pop up anywhere now and if you find Perennials such as Dock or Bramble aim to dig the roots out as well.

-If the weather has turned dry, aim to water plants each day.

-Continue to cut out excessive growth on Raspberries and tie in new shoots intended for fruiting next year.

-Prune cordon Gooseberries back to five leaves, and harvest fruits regularly and evenly along the stems.

-Early fruiting Raspberries, once all the fruit have been picked. Trim back to ground level.

-Harvest ripened Strawberries regularly and peg down runners you want for new plants, if not, trim these off.

-Apples may begin to naturally drop young fruits, there is no need to worry. Clear away the fallen fruit and if branches are heavily laden, thin out to space around 4 inches apart. Also, remove any diseased looking fruit and discard

-Now is the best time to Summer prune Red and

White currants. Do not cut back main shoots, instead trim any side shoots to leave five leaves from the base.

-Continue to tie in new shoots of fan trained plants.

-Thin all heavy cropping fruit trees to prevent branches snapping.

TREES & SHRUBS.

-Cuttings can be taken of plants such as Philadelphus, Ceanothus and Lavender. Take tip cutting of about 3 to 4 inches, remove the bottom leaves then cut below leave joint. Dip the end in hormone powder and pot up in a gritty compost. Cover with a clear polythene bag and leave in a shaded area. Cuttings should be rooted in about 6 to 8 weeks.

-Continue pruning Spring and Summer flowering shrubs after flowering such as Philadelphus and Ribes. To promote thick growth and avoiding woody stems aim to prune back by a third. With doing this each year it will prevent the leaves becoming smaller and promote better flowering

-Keep an eye on newly planted trees and shrubs for drying out and water regularly.

-Keep Privet, yews and Lonicera hedges tidy by pruning long new shoots.

-Summer cuttings are a great way to increase your plants for free. By following these simple rules, you can easily increase your plants. Only select healthy shoots free from disease. Don't let them dry out, or over compacting the compost excluding air. Never leave them waterlogged and inspect them regularly. Always use fresh compost to prevent diseased compost infecting your cuttings. Dip in a hormone powder to increase the chances of a cutting striking. Pinch out any flowering buds to conserve the cutting's energy in producing roots. Some plants worth trying are Abelia, Azalea, Ceanothus, Choisya, Cistus, Cotoneaster, Euonymous, Forsythia, Hebe, Hibiscus, Hypericum, Ilex Lavatera, Potentilla, and Weigela just to name a few.

-Bulbs grown in the spring such as Tulips and Daffodils can now be cut back, dig up and begin drying for next season.

THE GREENHOUSE.

-Daily check for watering and pests such as Red spider mite, White fly and Vine weevils, Biological controls are available by mail order.

-Tomatoes need growing tips tied in and side shoots removing.

-Cucumbers will need the tip pinching out once it has reached the top of its support.

-Continue to shade plants to prevent sun scorch.

-Ventilate the greenhouse each morning and close on chilly nights and check plants that need watering each morning.

-Damp down the greenhouse floor each morning.

-Mist Cucumber plants to keep the humidity high

and deterring Red Spider Mite.

THE POND.

- Keep removing blanket weed to prevent it taking over your pond.
- Keep an eye on water levels and top up when necessary, avoid adding tap water direct from the main as the nitrates can promote algae blooms. Use rainwater or store tap water in containers to allow the nitrates to disperse naturally then add to your pond.
- Continue planting new aquatic plants. They will establish quickly this month and remember to sprinkle a layer of gravel over new plants in baskets to prevent the compost being disturbed.
- Clean pumps regularly to prevent blockages.
- Ponds with fish will need feeding more regularly when temperatures rise but be careful not to over feed.
- Fountains and waterfalls need to be kept running in hot spells to keep the water oxygenated for your fish.
- Aim to complete all new planting this month so that plants have time to establish.

- Continue to weed your rock gardens and replace tired looking plants. Redress the gravel to keep it looking fresh.

LAWN CARE.

- Continue to cut lawns at least once a week, pref-

erably twice.
-Apply a fertiliser to help boast your lawn
-Continue to spot treat weeds.
-If bare patches appear, scarify then sprinkle on a seed and compost mix and protect for birds. Water regularly until established.
-Remove a build-up of lawn thatch using a lawn rake.
-Trim untidy edges using an edging iron.

FOOD PLANTS FOR BUTTERFLIES.

All of us love nothing better than spotting butterflies in our gardens so here is a list of plants for you to consider putting in your garden to attract them. Like many creatures once mating is done, they are looking for a place to lay their eggs for the larva to feed on.

Couch grass, Meadow-grass, Alder buckthorn, Elm, Hop Stinging Nettles, Thistles, Cock's Foot, Broom, Bents, Fescues, Yorkshire fog, Holly, Ivy, Dogwood, Dock, Sorrel, Nasturtiums, Cabbage, Birds foot trefoil, Red Clover, Tormentil, Rest Harrow, Charlock, Honesty, Sweet Rocket Lady's Smock, will attract butterflies such as Ringlet, Brimstone, Comma, Red Admiral, Painted Lady, Peacock, Speckled Wood, Large Skipper, Small Tortoiseshell, Holly Blue, Small Copper, Wall Brown, Large White, Common Blue, and Orange Tip into your garden.

AUGUST.

The Summer Months can often be the busiest time of year in the garden and with holiday season well underway, preparation is needed to be made to ensure your precious plants are still tended for. Mulching around plants and providing shading will all help to conserve moisture while you are away. Many plants will have reached their peak and need dead heading regularly. Your vegetable and fruiting plants will also be cropping well by now and will also need to be cared for if you are away for long periods of time. A good neighbour can be your best asset at this time of year with helping you out with watering. Remember, while your garden is at its peak do go out and actually enjoy it. It's not all work, work, work.

HOLIDAY TIPS.

-Indoor plants can suffer badly if you are away for two weeks so before leaving, move them away from sunny windows. Grouping larger plants together will also help and standing them on trays with damp gravel.

-You can group smaller plants on the kitchen

A GENERAL GUIDE TO FILLING YOUR GARDEN WITH

drainer or in the bathtub. Using a capillary matinglinked to a slow dripping tap will help to keep them watered.

-By far the best way to look after your plants is to ask a neighbour to come around and check on them, and if possible, give your outdoor plants a watering as and when needed.

-When you have returned from holiday give all your houseplants a liquid feed.

FLOWERS.

-Keep dead heading Roses but leave varieties that are valued for their rose hips. Continue to spray susceptible varieties against Mildew, Rust and Blacks pot, continue to remove any suckers.

-Keep dead heading your potted plants and hanging baskets to prolong flower displays. Aim to do this before seed sets. Water regularly, feed with a high pot ash fertiliser weekly and water daily during hot dry spells.

-Continue taking cuttings to increase plant stocks.

-Pansies and Violas raised in August by taking cuttings can be potted on in sandy compost.

-Continue taking cuttings from shrubs.

-Continue providing support for tall flowering plants and tie in regularly.

-Wisteria can be Summer pruned by shortening side shoots to 6 inches.

-Violas and Pansies that have been cut back last month, use the new growth for cutting.

-Hydrangeas that have finished flowering can be pruned back to a healthy pair of leaves. Leave flower heads on if you are in a frost prone area to protect the plant.

VEGETABLES.

-Crops to sow directly outside this month are Beetroot, Cabbage, Carrots, Chinese Cabbages, Endive, Lettuce and Spring Onions.

-Pick Broad Beans regularly and leave a few pods on the plant if you want to save seed, ensure they are non-hybrid varieties.

-Shallots can be harvested once their leaves start to bend and yellow. Leave outside once picked to dry for a day or two before collecting.

-Runner beans tips can be pinched out once they reach the top of their supports. Pick regularly to promote continual production.

-Moisture loving Celery must be kept watered well. Self-blanches varieties can be left alone but nonself blanching varieties need a collar tie to help to blanch the stems. Then earth can be mound up around the plants.

-Lift main crop Potatoes as soon as the top foliage turns yellow and started to die back.

-Keep an eye on Brassica crops for caterpillar attacks, remove as necessary.

-Thin out seedlings planted early to correct spacing.

-Continue picking salad crops while they are young and tender.

A GENERAL GUIDE TO FILLING YOUR GARDEN WITH

-Crops raised in seedbeds such as Leeks, Broccoli, Brussels Sprouts, Cabbages and Kale can be moved to their final growing bed.

FRUIT.

-Harvest fruits at their peak such as Strawberries, Raspberries, Currants, Blackberries and Cherries.

-Pears can be summer pruned now. Prune so that all side shoots are shortened back to six leaves.

-All Apple varieties should be pruned over the next few weeks. All long side shoots growing from the main branches should be shortened back to 6 inches and any short ones back to an inch. Tie in the tips of fan trained trees.

-Peaches and Nectarines need to be thinned to allow the remaining fruit to ripen.

-Continue to water in dry spells.

-Spray plants to control Mildew and Sawflies.

-If you have not already done so, thin out heavily laden fruit trees to prevent branches breaking and pick fruits as they ripen.

-Raspberry canes should be cut to ground level that have carried this year's fruit and new canes tied in. Remove any unwanted growth. Autumn fruits varieties will need to be netted to protect the fruits from birds.

-Net Blackberries and tie in new canes.

-Plant out earlier rooted runners of Strawberries and remove the straw from beds. Trim back old growth.

-Begin pruning hedges to retain their shape. Use secateurs on larger leafed hedges to prevent unsightly looking leaves. After pruning, water well and mulch.

THE GREENHOUSE.

-Keep checking for pests and pick off any you find.
-Keep checking for mildew and disease and spray with a suitable fungicide.
-Tie in Tomato shoots and continue to remove side shoots. Harvest fruits as they ripen and after five trusses have formed, pinch out the tops. This allows the plant to be able to ripen the remaining fruit. Removing the lower leaves also aids ripening and allows air flow round the plant.
-Keep picking Cucumbers to encourage further flowers to develop.
-Weekly feed plants.
-Shade plants from sun scorch.
-Open all ventilation each morning and damp down. If the weather is really hot, leave a vent open at night to aid air circulation.
-Make room for cuttings that have been taken and provide shading for these from direct sunlight.

-Plant Autumn flowering bulbs such as Colchicums and Sternbergias.
-Support Lily bulbs and Gladiola. Keep watering in dry spells.
-Lily bulbs developing in leaf axils can be picked off and potted up to produce new plants.

A GENERAL GUIDE TO FILLING YOUR GARDEN WITH

-Prepared Hyacinth bulbs will be in garden centres now, pot up straight away for Winter blooms.

-Continue mowing regularly and if dry spells persist move the mower height up a notch.

-Repair patchy lawns by reseeding and water newly laid lawns continually during dry spells to prevent shrinkage.

SEPTEMBER.

This month can feel like an extension to the summer with the weather still warm and the added delight that many fruits and vegetables are harvested this month. There is still plenty to do this month and some preparation for next year can begin. Bulbs can start to be ordered and dead heading flowers to keep shows going and leave a few flower heads for seed collecting, all will be well worth the effort.

FLOWERS.

-Begin sowing Hardy Annuals this month. Overwinter plants in the greenhouse and you will have an earlier display next year. First sow in trays then pot on, set out next year when the worst of the Winter weather is over.

-For a prolonged display in your pots and hanging baskets keep dead heading and feeding displays.

-Clematis stem cutting can be taken. Insert into compost and root on in the greenhouse or cold frame.

-Continue to cut spent flowers on Perennials unless you require them for seed collection.

A GENERAL GUIDE TO FILLING YOUR GARDEN WITH

-Continue to take cutting of tender Perennials. They should form a strong root system at this time of year and can be overwintered in the greenhouse.

-Allow foxgloves to disperse seed before cutting back to allow for next year's plants to self-seed.

-With the soil still warm now is a good time to plant out pot grown Perennials and Bi-annuals. Young plants will still have time to put on new growth and establish themselves before Winter.

-Prune Pelargoniums back hard to encourage new growth that can be used to take cuttings next month.

VEGETABLES.

-Onions can be lifted as soon as the leaves begin to bend over. Leave on top of the soil to ripen for a day or two. Order Onions set for Autumn.

-Leeks that need blanching, earth up soil around them.

-Beetroot is best harvest young for tastier roots.

-Lift maincrop Potatoes and second early and continue to water any left in the ground in dry spells.

-Celery variates that are not self-blanching will need collar ties and earthing up.

-Pick off any yellowing leaves on Brussels Sprouts to prevent disease.

-Plant out Spring Cabbages raised earlier into their final growing position.

-Marrows will be producing fewer blooms so select a few large fruits and keep off the soil with

a tile or brick. Trim excessive leaf growth if required to expose the Marrows to the full to ripen.
-Harvest salad crops regularly and while still young. Many will try to run to seed such as Lettuce so pick regularly.

FRUIT.

-Continue picking fruit as it ripens.
-As soon as Peaches have been all picked, prune the stems that carried the fruit hard back and tie in new season growth.
-Continue spraying against disease and if Aphids have become a problem, spray with a suitable insecticide.
-Start putting grease bands around Apple trees during this month to prevent the Winter moth from laying her eggs. Ensure the bands are a close fit around the tree.

-Finish pruning hedges at the end August and beginning of September to prevent early frost from damaging tender new shoots.
-Now is a good time to transplant evergreen shrubs. Prepare the new site first to minimise the time the root ball is out of the ground and add plenty of well-rotted compost. Heel in well and water regularly.

THE GREENHOUSE.

-Keep feeding Tomatoes and pick fruit regularly. Never let them dry out to prevent fruit problems.

- Keep a check on plants for pests.
- Ventilate the greenhouse during the day and close at night.
- Regularly check on cuttings, do not over water and remove any that have begun to show signs of disease.
- Shading may be removed to allow good sunlight in, ensure the temperatures are not to excessive on hot days to avoid sun scorch.

- Start ordering your Spring bulbs.
- Continue potting up prepared Hyacinths.
- Lilies can be planted now for flowering next year. If you are planting outdoors, ensure the soil is free draining and well-prepared.
- You can start planting Spring bulbs now. Begin planting Crocuses, Daffodils, Hyacinth, Scillas and Winter Aconites. Delay planting Tulips until October and early November.

LAWN CARE.

- During dry spells higher the blades on your mower by one notch.
- Do not feed lawns with a high Nitrogen feed, instead use a fertiliser designed for Autumn feeding.
- This month is a good month to sow or lay new lawns. Prepare the ground as previously mentioned in May's lawn care section.

OCTOBER.

This month sees in the Autumn in earnest, but the garden can still be a riot of colour as the trees begin to put on their Autumn leaf colour displays. The first frosts illuminate the garden in a magical display, with spider webs standing out like silver netting trailing between plants. There is still plenty of jobs to do, and this month is a good time to evaluate your borders to see what has given you a good show and make notes of plants that have not done so well that need to be replaced or moved. Beds that have been cleared can begin to be dug over where needed, and late fruit crops need to be harvested and prepared for storing.

FLOWERS.

-Now is the time to start thinking about putting many tender plants to bed for the Winter and before the frosts arrive. Acting now will save many of your plants being damaged by sudden overnight freezing temperatures.

-Bring all tender potted plants into a frost-free place.

-Potted plants that remain outside will need to

be lagged to protect the root ball from prolonged freezing temperatures.

-Cut back any Perennials that have finished flowering.

-Annuals can be dug up that have succumbed to early frosts.

-Lightly fork over borders that have been cleared and apply a mulch.

-Tender Perennials need to be lifted and store to prevent the worst of the Winter weather damaging them.

-Dahlias can be lifted as soon as the first frosts turn the leave brown. Cut back to 6 inches and hang them upside down for a few days to dry out. Plunge the tubers into a sandy mix and keep dry and in a frost-free place.

-Bare rooted Roses can start to be planted. Before planting, prune the Roses to shape cutting above outward facing buds. Trim roots to encourage good new strong growth and apply a generous amount of well-rotted compost. Heel in well and water.

VEGETABLES.

-Start planting Onion sets and Garlic Bulbs.

-Start collecting seed catalogues at your local garden centre or write off to the seed companies for them and see what new varieties are on offer for next year.

-Start preparing beds for next season. Dig over and manure beds for next year's Beans, Capsicums, Celeriac, Cucumbers, Endive, Leaf Beet, Leeks, Lettuce, Marrows, Onions, Peas, Spinach, Sweetcorn and tomatoes. Rake in gardening lime for Cabbages, Cauliflowers, Swedes, Khol Rabi and other Brassicas.

-Dug up and divide crowed Rhubarb clumps at the end of this month. Ensure they have plenty of new buds and replant in well-prepared soil.

-Sow early varieties of Broad Beans and Peas. Sow directly into prepared beds and cover with cloches. Alternatively, sow in pots in the greenhouse to plant out in a few weeks. Ensure you plant them in a sheltered location away from chilling winds and a free draining site. Stake cloches to prevent them being blown over.

FRUIT.

-Continue to pick Apples and Pears and any other fruits still ripening.

-New Raspberry canes can be planted this month. Plant 12 to 18 inches apart leaving a 12-inch stem above ground.

-Continue to prune out fruited canes of Blackberries.

-Continue to prepare sites for planting new fruiting trees and bushes, cover the soil to keep it workable if delayed.

-This month is a good time to plant a new hedge. Many bare-rooted hedges will be available, and the cheaper prices may work out better for longer hedges. Prepare the soil well, incorporating plenty of organic matter and apply a bone meal dressing when growth begins in the Spring.

THE GREENHOUSE.

-Remove all greenhouse shading this month to maximise sunlight. Giving the glass a clean will also help.

-Check plants for overwintering pests, treat as necessary

-Tomatoes that have finished fruiting need to be removed to prevent overwintering pests being harboured. Any green Tomatoes can be removed and ripened on a sunny windowsill.

-Any other cropping plants that have finished producing crops should also be removed.

-Tulips are best planted this month.

-Lilies that are still becoming available in garden centres can be propagated from the scales. Remove healthy scales and plant to half their depth in soil less compost.

LAWN CARE.

-Scarify lawns that have accumulated a thatch over the Summer months and apply an Autumn feed.

-Adjust the height on your lawn mower to the maximum height.

-If frosted, keep off lawn to prevent damage.

-Begin raking off Autumn leaf fall.

-If damp weather persists, resist mowing your lawn until the weather is dry. This will save your lawn looking a mess and prevent your lawn mower being clogged up by damp clippings.

NOVEMBER.

Now that Winter is looming once again a lot more of the gardening time will be dedicated to keeping it tidy and preparing for next year. Recycling leaf litter and removed spent plants to add to the compost heap will reap you rewards of barrows full of free nutrient rich compost. Remember to keep protecting those tender plants and bring into a sheltered spot free from frost. Collecting all those leaves can be well worth the effort once you see it turn into a lovely leaf compost and is a handy soil conditioner and mulch, for free.

FLOWERS.

-Continue to dig up dahlia tubers for storing.
-Dry out tubers such as Begonias, Gloxinias, and Achimenes. Remove from their pots and clean off the compost. Dust with Sulphur powder and store in paper bags in a cool dry frost-free place.
-Continue to plant bare-rooted Roses.
-Winter flowering hanging baskets can be planted up now. Lining the basket with moss will help retain moister and protect the roots. Check for watering regularly and hang in a sheltered spot

out of wind.

-Aim to finish lifting all your tender plants before the Winter cold sets in.

-Complete sowing of Sweet Peas in pots to be kept in the greenhouse or cold frame.

-Finish planting out Winter and Spring bedding plants such as Pansies, Primulas, Wallflowers and Forget-me-nots.

-Begin collecting seeds. Choose a dry day and prune the entire seed head. Keep in a paper bag with the seed head hanging upside down to allow the seeds to drop to the bottom of the bag. Seeds in husks or pods can be separated once they are completely dry. Label and place in an airtight container, then store in a dark cool place.

-Continue to prick out hardy Annuals as soon as they are ready.

-Keep collecting fallen leaves around Roses and if they show signs of disease don't add these to your compost heap. Keep ordering bare-rooted Roses until February.

-Continue dividing Perennials that are congested or looking tired. Save healthy parts and replant in well-prepared soil.

-Alpine beds need to have fallen leaves cleared away to prevent overwintering pests such as slugs and snails hiding under them.

-Collect all support canes no longer in use, clean and store for next season.

VEGETABLES.

A GENERAL GUIDE TO FILLING YOUR GARDEN WITH

-Continue planting Onion sets and Garlic Bulbs.

-Start collecting seed catalogues at your local garden centre or write off to the seed companies for them and see what new varieties are on offer for next year.

-Start preparing beds for next season. Dig over and manure beds for next year's Beans, Capsicums, Celeriac, Cucumbers, Endive, Leaf Beet, Leeks, Lettuce, Marrows, Onions, Peas, Spinach, Sweetcorn and tomatoes. Rake in gardening lime for Cabbages, Cauliflowers, Swedes, Khol Rabi and other Brassicas.

-Dug up and divide crowed Rhubarb clumps. Ensure they have plenty of new buds and replant in well-prepared soil.

-Sow early varieties of Broad Beans and Peas. Sow directly into prepared beds and cover with cloches. Alternatively, sow in pots in the greenhouse to plant out in a few weeks. Ensure you plant them in a shelter location away from chilling winds and a free draining site. Stake cloches to prevent them being blown over.

FRUIT.

-Continue to pick Apples and Pears and any other fruits still ripening.

-New Raspberry canes can be planted this month. Plant 12 to 18 inches apart, leaving a 12-inch stem above ground.

-Continue to prune out fruited canes of Blackberries.

-Continue to prepare sites for planting new fruiting trees and bushes, cover the soil to keep it workable if delayed.

TREES & SHRUBS.

-Now is a good time to take hardwood cuttings from plants such as Currants, Gooseberries, Weigela, Willows, Roses, Poplars, Privet, Forsythia, Buddleia just to name a few.

-Continue to move shrubs you want to relocate and as mentioned in October, dig the new hole first adding plenty of organic matter.

-Aim to complete Conifer hedge pruning this month.

-Order your new trees and shrubs for Winter and Spring planting.

-Check tree ties after windy weather, tighten or replace if required.

-Dry out Gladiola corms for storing.

-Aim to complete all Tulip and Spring bulb planting.

THE GREENHOUSE.

-Keep checking for pest.

-Ventilate the greenhouse in the afternoons on sunny days to conserve heat.

-Keep conditions for overwintering plants such as Geraniums completely frost free and water minimally. Take off any foliage that is dead or yellowing to prevent disease.

-Stop watering bulbs overwintering in pots and allow the foliage to die back.

-Check heaters daily from now on.

-If you have not already done so, clear out all Tomatoes and crops in pots and grow bags. Add the foliage to the compost heap and consider using the spent compost for soil conditioning your soil.

THE POND.

-Leaf fall will need to be collected regularly from the surface of ponds. A simpler way is to use netting pegged over the top of your pond to collect the leaves before they sink to the bottom.

-Remove water pumps and filters. Clean thoroughly for storing until next year.

LAWN CARE.

-The lawn can still be mown if it is still growing well but remember to higher the blades on your mower.

-Keep off lawns in very wet weather and frosty mornings. As with last month, only mow on dry days and avoid mowing in the morning with dew on the lawn.

-To make leaf collecting easier, set your mower to its highest setting and use it to collect the leaves. This also shreds the leaves and will aid in decomposition when added to your compost heap.

DECEMBER.

December is probably the hardest month of the year to feel like going outside into the winter weather and do some gardening. Christmas and the new year need to be planned for and the garden is probably the last thing on your mind. There are still jobs to be done and with some planning ahead now you can be enjoying early crops and blooms. Bulbs planted out earlier will soon be rewarding your efforts and with some careful planting choices there is still a lot of colour to be seen.

FLOWERS.

-If you have lifted and potted up half-hardy perennials and put them under cover or in the greenhouse, they will need extra protection this month during prolonged spells of cold.

-Herbaceous plants left in the ground may need protecting, so if you are unsure if they are hardy then mulch around roots, paying particular attention to cover round crowns.

-Now is a good time to go through seeds catalogues and decide on what plants you intend to grow next year.

A GENERAL GUIDE TO FILLING YOUR GARDEN WITH

-Hardy plants to sow in the greenhouse next month are Pansies, Antirrhinums, Violas, Cornflowers.

-Roses can be tidied up and any leggy stems reduced by half to prevent wind damage in readiness for pruning in March. Collect any leaves under rose bushes to prevent black-spot overwintering.

-Summer Annuals like Pelargoniums, Sweat Peas, and Begonias can be sown next month so plan ahead to ensure you have all you need. A heated propagator or sunny windowsill will be required for germination.

VEGETABLES.

-If you are looking to grow a large Onion variety, now is the time to plan for next month's planting.

-Early varieties of Potatoes can be potted up next month so ensure you have all you need. Also, order seed Potatoes now for planting out in March.

-Many crops are still in season such as Beetroot, Brussels sprouts, Cabbage, Carrots, Onions, Parsnips, Potatoes and Shallots, and Pigeons can cause a lot of damage to winter greens. Cover with mesh or netting to prevent damage.

-Early hardy Pea and Broad bean sown now will need protecting from prolonged cold spells with cloches.

-If you have stored vegetables, check regularly for rot and disease, dispose of to prevent it spreading to other crops.

-Cabbage roots should be cleared away straight

after harvest to prevent harbouring pests and disease which could infect crops later on in the year.

-Now is good time, if you have not already done so to dig over and manure your vegetable plot in preparation for planting time.

-Parsnip beds can be prepared now. Dig over, removing large stones and dig in fine organic material to prevent roots forking.

-Rhubarb will benefit from a thick layer of well-rotted manure. If you want to force some young tender shoots, then place a large terracotta pot over the crown.

FRUIT.

-Now is a good time to apply a Tar wash to your fruit trees to protect them against overwintering disease spores and kill off pests. Pay attention to all the nooks and crannies that may harbour pests and disease.

-If you have fruit cages, remove netting to prevent it being damaged by heavy snow.

-Peach trees can have a copper fungicide applied now and protect them against rain splash in Winter to prevent peach leaf curl disease.

-Pot grown plants can be brought into the greenhouse now to encourage early growth.

-Vines can be pruned. Shorten side shoots to 1 or 2 buds from the main stem.

-Protect Gooseberries and Currents with netting to prevent birds stripping off the new buds.

-Blueberries will benefit from a generous mulch of

A GENERAL GUIDE TO FILLING YOUR GARDEN WITH

high acid compost.

-Cherry trees can be difficult to protect fruit on large specimens. By selecting a tree that has been grafted on a dwarf root stock can be easily protected with netting to protect fruit. Do check you have selected a self-fertile variety, but if you plan to plant more than one then the choice of varieties is greatly increased.

-Continue planting fruit trees and bushes.

TREES & SHRUBS.

-Deciduous trees and shrubs can be pruned now when weather permits this to be done, they can also be planted out into their permanent position when weather permits.

-Heavy snow should be knocked of evergreens to prevent damage.

-Trees and shrubs can be planted out now. Prepare the ground well and dig deeply mixing in fertiliser and if the soil is in a poor condition add compost. If conditions are very wet and cold it will be better to wait until the weather improves. Try to complete all bare rooted trees, shrubs and roses by March, before the plants come back into growth.

-Check newly planted trees and shrubs after hard frosts and heel in if necessary, to firm the ground around the root ball.

-Before growth begins, pollarded trees can be pruned to keep them within manageable size.

-If rabbits are a problem, protect new trees with

wire mesh or trunk bands to prevent lower bark being chewed off.

BULBS.

-Keep a check on pot grown bulbs and do not allow them to become waterlogged or too dry. Protection will be needed during long spells of cold weather.

-Lilies can be potted up now to be planted out later when the weather improves.

-At this time of year many outlets will be selling bulbs cheaply to clear stocks, so if you did not manage to buy and plant them out in the Autumn, there is still time to grab a bargain and pot them on in the greenhouse to be planted out later on.

-If you are looking for colour in your garden at this time of year there is a surprising amount to choose from and none easier to grow than from bulbs such as Aconite, Cyclamen, Anemones, Crocus, Iris and Narcissus have all early varieties to choose from and are a welcome early splash of colour.

THE GREENHOUSE.

-If you have not already, your greenhouse would benefit from a good clean down. It is surprising how much light algae on the glass can prevent good quality light from entering. With soapy warm water and a squeegee on a nice day, it is a satisfying job to do and will benefit you later on when you start sowing again. It also a good time to clean all those used pots and have a general tidy up to prevent overwintering pests building up and feasting on any plants you intend to grow on later in the spring.

-Conserve heat in the greenhouse by lining the inside with bubble wrap.

-Cold frames will also benefit from a clean and general tidy ensuring the glass is clean and the lid is fully working.

-Overwintering Alpines will need good ventilation in the greenhouse, weather permitting, but do keep out damp air.

-Now is a good time to ensure heaters and propagators are working correctly.

-Clear snow off greenhouses and cold frames to improve light levels.

-When weather permits, ventilate greenhouse to ensure a good supply of air is circulated to prevent the build-up of harmful moulds which can rot stems and leaves.

-Water plants sparingly in the morning to allow plants to dry out before night-time frost can harm your plants. A spray bottle is ideal for this to help prevent overwatering. If you do overwater a plant, tap out of pot and leave to dry out. Re-pot as soon as the plant begins to dry out.

-Ensure all maintenance of the greenhouse is done and replace broken panes of glass if necessary.

-If you have potted up Chrysanthemums, once flowering is finished cut back to 12 inches from the base.

THE POND.

-Ice is the problem to keep an eye out for this month. Use a pan of hot water placed on the ice to melt a breath hole for fish. Frogs can also overwinter in ponds and also will need to breath. Do not be tempted to break the ice because the shock wave could startle fish and kill them.

-Herons can be a welcome visitor to your garden, but they will be looking for lunch. Where you can prevent losses, is by placing a terracotta ridge tile, or pipe into the pond to give your fish a hiding place.

-If snow falls during spells on your pond when being frozen, this can prevent light getting through. Clear off snow as soon as possible.

THE ROCK GARDEN.

-At this time of year your Alpines will benefit from a top dressing of gravel or shingle to help protect them from severe wet weather. As mentioned in January, redress any waterlogged areas.

LAWN CARE.

-In heavy spells of snow try to avoid piling this onto your lawn as this can damage the lawn underneath, also avoid walking when it is frosted.

-If you are planning a new lawn in the spring now is a good time to prepare the ground and allow time for the soil to settle before laying or seeding the new lawn.

A GENERAL GUIDE TO FILLING YOUR GARDEN WITH

-Avoid walking on the lawn during spells of heavy frost.

-During heavy spells of rain you may find areas of your lawn that are water logged, make a note of these areas and correct later in the year by either air-rating by spiking the area, or if the area is seriously water logged then a drainage system may need to be implemented.

GENERAL GARDEN CARE.

-Continue, on those dry days, racking up the remaining leaves that have fallen. Your lawns will also be looking not at their best and it could be tempting to bring the lawn mower out on a nice day, this is definitely not a good idea. The frosts will damage the grass and make it look worse.

-Areas where you intent to sow early crops will benefit from being covered with polythene or old carpet to help warm the soil in readiness later on.

-Weather permitting, your borders can be tidied up now. Clear leaves and twigs then lightly fork over the area.

-The compost heap will benefit from being turned over now. Dig thoroughly, incorporating the different layers and breaking up any clumped together material. Cover with polythene or an old carpet to continue decomposing.

-The winter months can be particularly harsh for wildlife with prolonged spells of the garden being frozen solid. Birds will not be able to forage easily, and hibernating insects can be killed off by the cold.

-Check bird feeders and tables daily and remove frozen water from bird baths. A good tip for saving cost on bird seed is to buy larger sacks of seed. This with work out cheaper than buying smaller bags and will ensure you have a plentiful supply because you will be surprised at how much seed will consumed at this time of year, especially during prolong spells of cold weather.

-When doing your garden clean up, spare a thought for earth worms. They consume many fallen leaves during the Winter so try not to be over rigorous in collecting every single leaf that has fallen.

-Moss in your lawn may be unsightly, but where you can, leave an area untouched and when you look out into your garden in the early morning you will see why. Many bird's species forage through the moss for insects and some collect it for nesting.

-If you have amassed a large amount of material during the winter to burn off now, move all the material to check to see if hedgehogs have used the area to hibernate inside.

If you do find this book helpful, then do please leave a review. I personally read them all and will always strive to make improvements to my books wherever possible. Many thanks and happy gardening, Andy.

http://www.amazon.co.uk/hp/B071ZTM5FK UK

A GENERAL GUIDE TO FILLING YOUR GARDEN WITH
http://www.amazon.com/hp/B071ZTM5FK US

Made in the USA
Lexington, KY
24 July 2019